The Grace of Dragons

The Grace of Dragons

Receiving the Gifts
of Dementia Care Partnering

by Lori Kane

The Grace of Dragons
Receiving the Gifts of Dementia Care Partnering

Cover by: Isaac Novak

ISBN-13: 978-0-9862996-5-0
ISBN-10: 0986299650

Lori Kane
www.collectiveself.com
Email: lori@collectiveself.com

Share feedback on the book at:
feedback@collectiveself.com

Printed by Createspace. An Amazon.com company.

For care partners, their partners,
and others learning to become their own respite

Contents

Her Name is Linda

My mom Linda was diagnosed with Alzheimer's disease by a doctor in 2007. She was just 60 years old. Mom, dad Jim, sister Jen, and I all knew that something was going seriously wrong with Mom for several years before that diagnosis. Memory troubles showed up. Anxiety and depression showed up. All new to her. More significant personality changes, such as not wanting to talk on the phone with us anymore, not wanting to visit Jen and me anymore, not wanting to do many of her favorite things, and avoiding spending time with other family members, friends, and large groups of any kind. She began spinning in worry about simple things, such as spending hours worrying that she would forget to feed the dog at 4 p.m. In those early years, worry spinning began causing her to repeat herself: such as asking me 15 times, in 30 minutes, to make sure she didn't forget to take a bottle of water into the theater with her.

The more we read about the disease, the more we suspected Mom had Alzheimer's. Even so, it took us years to finally get her to the doctor for that official diagnosis. She was remarkably sly at avoiding that doctor visit, including cancelling appointments behind Dad's back: another completely-not-like-her thing to do.

Back then, I was terrified and felt utterly alone. I think we all did. And why wouldn't we? In my country almost nobody is in a rush to diagnosis this disease: not the people who have the disease, not the people who love them, and not even many of our doctors. As a country, this disease terrifies us.

Fast forward to the fall of 2015.

We are an entirely different being today: a collective being. Reflective and thoughtful. Calm within storms some days. Creator of storms other days. Able to drop worry, stress, fear, ego, and even people, if need be, in the blink of an eye. We're becoming quite the bad ass together. More fluid and funny too. I'm a creator now: writer, poet, artist. My sister recently became a mom. We even speak a wordless new language now. Speak collectively out of habit. From my perspective today, the difficulties we experienced before are mostly symptoms of trying to tackle change and chaos, and trying to fix unfixable problems, as lone individuals. The result of standing in a river alone and trying to make what is right now back into what used to be. How impossible and exhausting that was.

Some people receive long, healthy individual lives to become something more than they once were. Others, like us, receive and accept diseases like this: a disease that requires us to become something new, something different, and something more than individual selves each new day. This disease surfaces our collective selves. Our dragon selves. Our river selves.

So yes, as a dragon/river/human/community hybrid being, this disease doesn't terrify me now. Not anymore. Even though I myself may end up with it as soon as 10 years from now. *Thank you Alzheimer's.*

In August I was sitting outside a coffee shop, in the warm sun, having lunch with a friend who is also an Alzheimer's care partner. In addition to talking about our marriages, food, the wild world of indie authoring and self-publishing, our mid-life aspirations, and our families, he brought up the subject of euthanasia. We talked about when and if our loved ones might make that choice and when and if we, ourselves, would ever make that choice. I've never had this conversation with anyone: not my husband, my parents, or my sister. It was a deep, lovely, moving, weird, and fascinating conversation, woven into and around talk of annoying husband quirks, great new food spots in the area, and the stubborn expansiveness of mid-life waistlines.

As I drove home, I realized that I'd just had yet another amazing, life-affirming conversation that I wouldn't have been strong enough to have before Alzheimer's disease entered my life. With a close friend I may not have had without this disease. And, even more amazing, that I'd just spontaneously taken a 4-hour lunch break out of the middle of a glorious, sunny work day. The old Lori would never have done that. Never. *Thank you Alzheimer's.*

This book is a collection of essays and poems that I wrote between 2012 and 2015 — the years my panic about Mom's disease had subsided enough for me to notice beauty again. Create beauty, anywhere and from anything. The essays and poems have been grouped in the book by one of the gifts they share in common, out of chronological order, so dates, times, and world events may seem a bit jumbled and confused. That's ok. In this world, the gifts are the focus. Everything else is background noise.

Thank you Alzheimer's.

The Six Gifts

The first time I looked back across the last four years of my essays and poetry, I found 16 gifts. But that's a lot of gifts to wrap a mind around and attempting to juggle them hurt my brain. So I breathed deeper, looked again, and just six gifts — my favorite gifts — surfaced. We've organized the book into five sections that reflect these gifts. The sixth gift shows up in the epilogue. For those inclined to look, there are other gifts to be found. For those who are busy, these are plenty.

1. Non-Fixing

In the land of problem fixers, the greatest teacher is an unfixable problem. We Alzheimer's care partners — and many others who dance within and around terminal and chronic illnesses — have been given an unfixable problem. The work in this section highlights my personal forays into learning about non-fixing. This gift is about doing nothing as a conscious practice for getting important things accomplished, mastering the ancient art of not giving a fuck, falling in love with what is again, and about allowing obstacles to become gifts. If this sounds cheesy and too self-helpy to you, so be it. I'm not fixing it.

2. Receiving Help from Everywhere

Dementia cracks care partners open. You know this. It can leave us wounded, raw, reeling, lost, and feeling what I imagine bleeding internally must feel like. The more cracked open we allow ourselves to become (and are forced to become, lucky us), the more help can pour in from everywhere: pets, poems, trees, cars, washing machines, seals, the ego, neighbors, pain, birds, silly cat videos, presence, poorly written erotica, clouds, crafting and creating, professionals, music, children, our own body, really bad TV, total assholes, and stars scattered across the night sky. Help can come to us from absolutely anywhere now. Anytime. We can learn to feel gratitude for the smallest thing — from a hint of a breeze on our faces to a cloud providing 10 seconds of relief from the heat. Fast-moving, closed-off, healthy, and/or perfection-seeking people often don't notice this reality for months, years, or even decades at a time. We, the broken wide open, can.

3. Fire, Peace, Courage

Some days with this disease are pure hell. Sometimes life sucks so bad and hurts so deeply that it feels like you are choking on smoke and burning in fire from within. There have been days, most recently when my extended family shattered, that I was sobbing for days at a time. I'm well aware now that there are days I would not survive without the help of close friends and family. I am the last person who will sugar coat this experience.

It was during a day when I was too mentally broken to even get out of bed that I began to notice the remarkable things about fire. Fire burns away what doesn't matter. Leaves what does. We — this disease, my closest family and friends, and I — stay with the fire, become it, and burn away the bad ideas and ridiculous crap that the adult world tries to pile on us daily. But it leaves us us. The us I recognize from childhood. The us capable of finding beauty everywhere, the us ok with not knowing, and the us who can shatter exquisitely, screaming into the night air as if the whole universe depended on it, like a 2-year-old might. We are becoming total bad asses together, which doesn't look anything like what a lone movie or TV bad ass looks like. In my world, being a bad ass means I can know myself, be myself, communicate and share what I need, anywhere. I can cry anywhere. Laugh anywhere. And I can comfortably allow others to do the same on their own terms, without freaking out about it. Much. Most days. Or I can join others in freaking out together, if that's what's needed by the moment. I am becoming someone who finds and creates peace — pulling poetry and essays into being, for example — even at the heart of the fire, the pain, the rage, and the despair. That's bad ass. And it's nothing more than being fully human in the way a cat is fully a cat or a dog is fully a dog.

Nobody is better positioned to make peace with being fully human than those who live with and near Alzheimer's disease and dementia.

Because we must live and move as community just to breathe. Just to get out of bed some days. And we regularly hold hands with fire together. As care partners we choose to stay with internal fire similar to the way I imagine a firefighter stoically walks into a burning building and for a similar reason: for the love of a community self. We care partners are burned by our daily choices until only our lovely, gentle, quiet, loud, and raging bad ass essence remains. Until we become both fire and the peace within. Become comfortable with both fire and peace in ourselves and in others in whatever form they happen to show up that day. From the outside, this may look like courage. From the inside, it's more like a daily, often subconscious, practice. The simple practice of falling in love with being human.

4. Sustained Creation

Alzheimer's disease didn't make me a creator. I was painting rocks and building sand castles (with frogs as royalty) on the beach long before Alzheimer's showed up in my life. But she did make me strong enough to recognize my adult self as a writer, poet, and artist. And she does regularly unleash sweeping waves of creativity within me. Slows me down into noticing how precious and short life is. Forces me to be present. Taps me into a river of sustained creation I didn't understand I was fully part of before. She fashions me into an unrecognizable-to-myself being capable of taking bigger risks. Has allowed me to take back wonder and awe to the point that I'm regularly noticing miracles again, like children do.

Alzheimer's has put fire into my hands: making me an editor capable of burning lovely but superfluous bits of writing to ash without shedding a tear. Toss out five lines or chapters or ideas or whole books and start again? Pffft. Child's play.

Alzheimer's morphs my family and neighbors into an improvisation troupe becoming ever more fluid (aka, not caring that we're awkward and clunky) at juggling love, pain, oddity, comedy, loss, and tragedy together. People aren't just people to me anymore. We are co-creators. And Alzheimer's isn't just Alzheimer's to me anymore either. Her name is Linda.

5. The Joy and Power of Groundless Beings

Where I live, we individuals often fear chaos and cling to order. Solid ground. I suspect it's because we were taught early, in school, that we are solid-ground-dwelling beings, born to thrive within order. This limited view of ourselves is bullshit, my friends. Lies. We are so much more than that.

Think about our imaginations. Given just four moments, you can be swimming in eerie dark waters with gray whales, then feel hollow excitement in your belly as you parachute out of a plane over that sea, then breathe in star dust while lounging in a hammock on the fine-dusted moon above, and wind up on another planet entirely, in tap shoes, tap dancing with purple beings beneath waving orange trees.

We are groundless beings, too. Dancers with chaos. Children show up to remind adults about the value of chaos and imagination. Sometimes we adults do so for each other as friends too. And people with Alzheimer's do this with all adults and children they encounter, including complete strangers. There is deep joy to be found within our groundless world for we soaring, groundless beings. We can dance across boundaries. We can cry anywhere. We can find fun anywhere. And the deepest joys often begin the very moment words fail us…

1. Non-Fixing

Becoming Magic With Her

I love Alzheimer's

when Mom looks into my eyes
says "My baby girl. I love you."
twinkles
hugs me close
she lifts the world to my lips
pours gratitude through me

inconsequential then
that names are dead
past is gone
old us drowned

we float happy here

no longer up to us to judge selves
fix others
worry needlessly
fret about what we don't have
who we aren't
carry world weight
harbor regret

we are free together
entirely
every moment I let us be

so I let us be

becoming magic with her

No More To-Do Lists and Other Joys of Turning 45

I turn 45 Sunday. This June baby moving toward June old lady. Last month my body began celebrating by throwing me hot flashes in lieu of a party. They're like a personal, internal fireworks show. So I'll be ringing in this birthday standing hot, alone, and naked outside on the deck, staring up at the stars at 3 a.m., trying to catch a breeze so I can go back to sleep. That may sound like a complaint but it's not. This new body? The one who demands I strip to sleep and insists that I move open-eyed and naked like an animal in the darkness in search of breeze on my face? I like her. I like her a lot. She makes being a poet a literal breeze.

Here at 45, I'm done sugar coating things for myself and others.

Here at 45, I am enough. Just me. Just here. Sans lists, most days. Without doing, fixing, stressing, worrying, or shopping to relax. Most days, I am enough now. Just me. The me that's drinking green tea and taking Evening Primrose Oil supplements to cool down, turning loose pieces of paper into makeshift fans, and rediscovering star-gazing, sweatily, in the middle of the night. In fact, I'm more than enough. Here at 45, I'm bad ass.

In part, because I have to be. As youth fades, you become invisible to many of the parts of the world that you cultivated before. I'm making peace with that. Learning to cultivate new worlds, new friends, new ways of being. Learning to be as content moving alone in the darkness as I am moving visibly, collectively with friends in the daylight.

I used to avoid giving advice like the plague. I'm not a fan of receiving unsolicited advice myself. Bleh. And, if you liked that me, this may not be the essay for you…

In the fire of family pain and the death of friends this year, I became a dragon and I burned my to-do lists to ash. My daily to-do list now isn't a list at all. It is two interwoven mantras:

- I Love You
- Fuck This

I say I Love You to the world, myself, and others as often as I can now. And I say Fuck This (or *Fuck That* or *Fuck It*, I like to mix it up) almost as often now too.

Beyond these mantras and my writing (where I get to play with these mantras in infinite variety) everything else I do now is icing on the cake: great when it happens, not so terrible when it doesn't.

At 45 I have failed. I have fallen apart. I have lost loved ones. I have broken down. I have looked like an idiot. I have not gotten nearly enough done. Regularly. I've learned that all these things are ok. I'm ok when they're happening (even while sobbing or screaming or yelling to cope). I'm ok after they've happened. Often better than ok. It's these things that have made me the bad ass that I am now: a person who fails, falls apart, receives loss, breaks down, looks like an idiot, doesn't get nearly enough done, says Fuck It, I Love You, laughs with friends and family, and moves on.

So yes, I offer advice on occasion now. Special occasions. Like my birthday. And here's my advice:

Say I Love You often.

Say Fuck This often.

There's my to-do list for now. Possibly my last list. Who knows?

Writer Anne Lamott would call these words *prayers*. You're welcome to do so, I Love You. And calling them prayers, for me, doesn't feel genuine, so Fuck It, that's not what I call them. For me they're mantras: words I repeat throughout the day to remind me of my true self, my deep connection to everything, and my own freedom to choose temporary disconnection in any moment, too. Some days I practice them. Some days they're habit within me and keep me present despite myself. To pull/push them toward being habit every day, I'm learning to involve my whole body in them. I try to hear myself say the words, when possible. Try to use appropriate gestures, too. Or do my own special dances or songs, to accompany the words, when possible. I try to be present enough to witness the rippling impacts of my doing so.

Here's one story from my life in which dragon-me burned away the To-Dos until only I Love You and Fuck This remain...

Every day I log in to the human world as an independent author: a world that is chaotic, loud, demanding, contradictory, and often unkind. It tells me to get an agent. To do book proposals. To make business plans. To go to an endless stream of conferences and work-shops and seminars and readings and networking events. To get professional credentials and degrees beyond the many I already have. To do proposals and pitches. To create an author platform. To live on social media, storytelling, and reader sites and to be relentlessly helpful and available there. To make friends with all local book sellers. To do in-bookstore readings. To visit book clubs. To teach. To grasp how to sell books and ebooks online on a dozen new and constantly shifting platforms. To read everything everybody else (who is really good) has ever written. To have a monthly newsletter. To work only with the best. To have perfect covers and keywords and descriptions and perfectly edited work and to pay for all this complementary ex-pertise to my own magically, somehow, out of pocket before I myself am making a living as an author. To get blurbs of praise to put on my book covers well ahead of time. To never include color images in books (and good God *never* include color images in poetry books). To ask more for my books. To ask less for my books. To give books away for free. To never give away books for free. To have an in-depth Press page. To finish and publish covers months ahead of time. To create art beyond the written word, which is, we're sorry, dead. To focus on just one genre and build deep community within one genre. To ignore genre, which is, we're sorry, also dead. To write for a cause. To never, ever write for a cause. And most importantly, to be writing every day, all the time, and do nothing else but write. A writer writes.

Enough, grownup world. Fuck This.

You know, I think I truly, deeply learned this technique by watching my mom, who has Alzheimer's disease, learn to do this first. She is a master. My own sweet Yoda.

With Fuck This' help, two years ago I moved to an island where I now spend days in silence each week and hours in nature each day. Huzzah! I spend three days alone writing most weeks. I spend one night a week talking and eating and relaxing with close women friends. I spend one or two days working side by side with my partner Daniel and one or two days relaxing each week. Or some variation of the above. Spending time with Mom and Dad, and helping them as needed, is like air to me now. Care partnering is woven into and around my weekly routine, as needed. Like breathing. It was my mom's, then my own, "Fuck This" that returned me to me. That returns me to I Love You.

Our Fuck This is wildly, uniquely our own and our I Love Yous look different too. Yet within us, they feel remarkably similar.

I Love You silence, trees, birds, whales, rocks, driftwood, wind, rain, sunshine, sand, warm days, sunsets, chilly nights, neighbors, making things with my hands, hanging out with family, coworking, and meeting my people: the random people wandering on beaches and in dog parks and creative indie humans and care partners scattered around the world.

I Love You reading and writing books. I Love You friends and family who help me create, share, gift, and sell books. I Love You self-publishing world that allows me to play with everything, including doing everything at a slow seasonal, tidal, poet's pace (and care partner's pace), and redefining what a book, a series, a genre, a writer, and an artist even is. I Love You humans willing to be human together. People who look at what being "An Expert" or "An Artist" or "A Perfect Parent" or "A Teacher" or "A Woman" or "A Caregiver" in the old world meant and say Fuck That.

I Love You, parents, who decided to move and join us here on the island, so we can all get exponentially better at saying both I Love You and also Fuck This, together.

When I wake up tonight at 3 a.m., in a puddle of sweat, neck on fire, I will begin by whispering Fuck This. Then I will rise, move out onto the deck into the night, look out at the ocean, up at the stars, and whisper I Love You.

We are one now — this ocean, these stars, and I — so one I Love You covers it.

And when one I Love You covers it, it becomes easier to say Fuck It to everything else.

Including to-do lists. Most days.

That's 45.

Stop Preaching Forgiveness to the Drowning
a poem for me

When you see a woman drowning
don't ask her to forgive the man beside her
throwing anchors in her direction.

You may be able to see that he is drowning too.
She can't. Plus,
forgiving him now will actually kill her.

Trust her deeper wisdom in this moment
her instinct to turn away.

For the love of God
stop preaching forgiveness to the drowning
when our only immediate options are turning away
or throwing anchors back and forth
until we drown.

Breaking Facebook Ties With
Beloved Family Members

Shit. I'm just getting to write about all sorts of fun stuff these days. Woo frickin' hoo, life, thanks. I'm not an expert on this subject, just somebody going through this pain right now.

When to unfriend somebody you love? pre-contempt

When you see that the next step you're most likely to take together will be feeling contempt for one another, and you don't want to go there, because you love each other, it's time to part ways for a while. You'll sense that if you don't step back now, take time to process pain and heal separately, that it's possible your relationship will never recover. Trust your intuition on this. Allow your heart and body intuition to override your guilt and your desire to fix things. The time to fix things is over. For now.

Signs that it's time to unfriend a loved one

- You are going through a drawn out, painful, heart-wrenching life transition. So are they.

- For them to survive and begin to heal, they need one story to be true right now. For you to survive and heal, you need a very different story to be true right now.

- When you share what you're feeling, you inadvertently hurt them, repeatedly. When they share what they're feeling, they inadvertently hurt you, repeatedly.

- That hurt begins to feel like it's on purpose. You begin regularly hearing meanness in what they say. And they hear it in what you say. Things that a stranger listening to you would never jump to such pain-fueled conclusions about. Your mutual pain is deep enough that you all begin to imagine slights that don't necessarily actually exist.

- Instead of being able to hold and see two or more equally valid perspectives, their truths become your lies, and vice versa.

- Every time you try to support one another, you fail miserably. It keeps getting worse, not better.

- When you speak your real, lived experience and perspective, you are told that you are wrong again and again and again. You never feel truly listened to or really heard.

- There is a wall of pain between you. You try repeatedly to holler over the wall that you really do see their side of things — and should be allowed yours — but it becomes clear that they're having the exact same experience that you're having (feeling that they're being told that they're wrong, feeling not listened to, not heard, and hurt by you).

- The existence of your story is too much for them to bear right now, and vice versa.

- You create and/or share something — a drawing, a painting, a poem, a song, a saying, a video, etc. — to help you and your closest others get even closer and move through your loss and grief together, and you learn that they were devastated by what you created/shared.

- You stop sharing your whole self, your true self, your real feelings — to protect them and yourself — to the point that you become exhausted, or get physically sick, because right now you really need to be able to share your whole self and your real feelings. And, in this case, Facebook is a place that you want to/used to be able to do that.

- You realize that time spent trying to hold up your old world/story/family together is unhealthy for everyone in your family. It is interfering with all of you finding and surrounding yourselves with the people you desperately need right now to create new worlds/stories/families for yourselves. Your heart breaks as you realize it's no longer each other that will help you heal.

My story

I wrote and shared a long poem on my blog (Hate Within Me Has a 3-Minute Shelf Life, which appears later in this book) about our family's struggle with Alzheimer's disease. We've lived with Alzheimer's in our family for 9 years now, and for the first time as a poet and a writer and a human, I felt ready to talk about pain more widely. More than that, I need to share about it that moment because my immediate family needed boatloads of new ideas, stories, help, support, and heart comfort as Mom moved into the middle stages of the disease, and my dad began crumbling under the weight of being a full-time primary caregiver.

And it worked. I got what we needed. Friends and strangers alike showed up to share their stories, offer their support, and surround our breaking hearts with love, light, understanding. I felt less alone. Less helpless.

And then I learned from my aunt that what I'd written was devastating for her and my uncles. My story too much for them to bear. A story out of alignment with their story. My truths are their lies. These are people I love to my deepest depths. People who helped raise me and played with me and who have loved me every day of my life. I adore them. And they live thousands of miles away, so Facebook has been the primary place where we've connected and shared for years now.

This aunt told me that she loved me but couldn't take any more of our pain right now, and she unfriended me. Letting me know that she'd reconnect later. I sat with that for a minute. Breathed it in. I, too, had "hidden" relatives this year that have been causing me chronic pain. But it had never dawned on me to unfriend them. When she did that, she freed both herself and me. I felt lighter and freer. I actually thought "Why didn't I think of that? Why did I stay in this masochistic situation for a year? She's a bloody genius!" I was reminded how much I love her. I followed her lead and unfriended a couple of uncles and a cousin — those who are being hurt by me and my story. Suddenly, after a year of trying to fix our family, I could just share my experiences without fear, and they could share theirs without fear! Hooray! I was at a point where I had to write about Alzheimer's disease and my experience of it. They were likely at a very painful point too. I wanted them to heal. I didn't want to cause them more chronic and inadvertent pain. That's not me. That's not us.

Example: how I unfriended a loved one

This is not advice. This is way too individual, personal, and painful a task for advice. This is simply what my aunt did for me and what I, in turn, did for the family members I unfriended. I'm sharing it because — although this was painful — in how we did it I also found a needed sense of closure (for now), peace, and a surprising freedom and lightness of spirit when I realized that I could, for the first time in a year, share my whole self again on Facebook. And I want the rest of my family to be able to do this too, for themselves, as needed. I want them to know that I'm 100% ok with them unfriending whomever they need to unfriend, including me, to heal.

In a private message, where I felt safe, I:

1. Reminded them that I loved them.
2. Told them I am sorry for their loss and pain.
3. In one sentence, I explained that I need to step away from them on Facebook right now so that I didn't inadvertently cause them pain again. I did not try to explain anything about my story/side, causing us more pain. The time for trying to be heard over the wall of pain had passed.
4. I reminded them that I loved them. So that the last words they received from me were words of love.
5. I unfriended them.

Different bits:

- If I felt the break was likely not forever, I told them so. In my aunt's case, she left it open ended. We'll be back in touch again someday. She reminded me that she's always still there if we really need her. I decided to give some of my relatives a time span. Said I'd disconnect for one year, while we went our separate ways to heal, and I hoped to reconnect with them again then.

- Because I still trust them, I gave them another way to connect with me if they really needed me. I gave them my email address, because that felt safest to me. If you don't want to do this, don't do it.

- Depending on the person, I gave them the option of re-engaging as Facebook friends down the line. I said to one person, for example: "I know what I'm going through is too hard for you to hear right now, so I'm unfriending you for a year. If, in the coming months you'd like to try reconnecting here, just send me a friend request and we'll try again if we're both ready." Whether or not you make this offer depends on your heart, not theirs. The state of your heart, and what you want, matters most here. If you want to be apart for a whole year (or more, or forever), don't make the offer to connect sooner.

What next?

Give yourself a long time to heal. For me, this unfriending family felt like cutting off my own hand. So I thought "How kind to myself would I be if I lost my hand? How long would I allow myself to heal and recover?" I decided that's how long I would be extra good to myself and surround myself with the best of the best heart-healers for me right now. That's how I came up with a year apart. I need at least that much healing time.

The actual act of unfriending someone takes one second, and so it could be mistaken for a little thing when it's not. Not if you love the people you're unfriending, and Facebook has been an important or only connection place for you. After you unfriend people you love, sit and breathe deeply for a while, go for a walk, hug someone or some furry beast who loves you or a tree (all of whom love you), create something, or do something else that brings you peace. Spoil yourself for a few days. Take comfort in the fact that you'll all have more energy and time to connect with people who will truly help you mend your broken heart without simultaneously also stomping on it.

In a workshop about fearless writing that I attended a while back, we began talking about writing memoirs. A memoirist in the class (I'm so sorry, I don't recall his name) said something so profound that I can't shake it. He said (and I'm paraphrasing) that the only pure, lasting truth in any family story is how people felt. To write fearlessly about your family, in a way that people will accept and connect with, you have to write and write, through many drafts, about how you felt. Don't allow yourself to stop when you are the victim in the story. Keep going. You must write and write and write until you become the protagonist – a spirit who others can relate to, see themselves in. Not a victim, not a braggart, but a life traveler, a story teller, a learner, a broken-heart survivor, a seeker of higher understanding. The things we all are. If you are writing yourself as a victim, keep writing, your story's not done.

When we make the decision to unfriend beloved family members on Facebook so that we can all heal, we're creating the opportunity for all parties to be able to come back again to that story one day on their own terms, with new found strength and abilities to stay with it longer next time, listen more closely next time, dig a little deeper next time, until we're able to craft and live a new story together. Or part as cherished friends.

The people we love deserve nothing less. Social media hasn't changed that.

Fall 2015 Addenda: I recently reconnected with three of the six family members I parted ways with a year ago when I first wrote this. Love does amazing things when we allow it to, doesn't it? Both in the coming back together as new friends and in remaking us into beings capable of truly letting some people to go with fondness and gratitude for the time we did have together.

The Return

I

Goodbye family who cannot bear the weight of me.
Goodbye family whose deep pain my own frame cannot bear.

We hung on for so long to outdated expectations
to what we used to be
failing each other, sinking our intertwined souls
until it sickened, almost killed
our right-now selves.
Thank God for chocolate.

Goodbye family

It says something remarkable about what we used to be
that we held on to old hopes and selves for so long

It says something more remarkable about what we are now
that we chose to breathe deep and let go here

Goodbye

We're finally free
to love what we still have more deeply
push away what no longer serves us
pull new love toward us
connect with other broken hearts better suited to heal our own.

II

Hello love

I love the faces that show up to listen and say "me too"
I love the earth that steadies my feet,
the thick fuzzy socks that warm them
I love the bed,
inviting judgement-free comfort zone, for the reminder

I love the cocoa for its short, sweet glimpse at days gone by

I love the power in the simplest of words now:
PJs rock. Fuck pants today.

I love the gathering power within.

I love the sky even more now
where thoughts float
among stars and words drop in like neighbors
I love neighbors
who stop by unannounced without words
like rock stars

I love that the sun never fails to warm my face
when I turn toward her.
I love that the family still beside me, smiling, able to cry my tears,
has become more powerful than the sun.

Hello love

I'm so glad we set down the weight of our own expectations
to race across the sand with the dog.
Yes, I was wearing pajamas.

I'm so glad we moved within pain to greet the new self approaching.
This broken-hearted, love-rich, weeping bad ass.
This never-not-broken goddess,
sleepy and tireless, strong and vulnerable
defender of broken-hearted people and their worlds.

I'm so glad we all remember with body-deep clarity
what a loving family feels like.

I'm thrilled that none of us settles for less
for ourselves and those we love.

I love that you have so much strength and fight left in you
that you'll be just fine, free and rising, without us.

III

Goodbye family, I love you

Thank you for teaching me to love
when I was little.

Thank you for learning with me
now that we're grown
that we won't settle for less
from anyone.

Thank you for bravely pulling forth your unspoken so I could see it.

IV

The girl you knew
Drowned
in a sea of frustration, half-truths,
rage, fear, and assumptions.
She is dead.
Mourn her as long as you need to.
Then let her go.

V

When you are ready, come

Come greet the woman
who steps toward you from the sea
laughing, wounded, new, content, scarred, and whole.
Sacred truths shatter around her. She doesn't.
(Ok, sometimes she does shatter before she rises.)
Love never leaves her presence.
She's a wellspring of love
because love shows up in others, surrounds her
pours into her when she's nearing empty
and she lets it all in

She loves messiness and openness. Leaves sand on the floor.
Dishes go unwashed for days sometimes.

She sleeps late.
Visiting friends learn to make their own breakfast.
She's been seen walking barefoot in the sand, even in winter.
She pulls rainbows out of the darkest sky
from bed, in her pajamas, while crying.

She may be strange but she's not a stranger.
She has her mother's smiling eyes.
She may be fierce sometimes
and there's absolutely nothing to fear within her.
Her father's strength.

You will find rest and welcome at her shore.

Bring comfy pajamas. Wash your own dishes. Forgive.
And you'll be invited to return.

2. Receiving Help from Everywhere

Talking With Neighbors

I was telling my neighbor how much I appreciate the multigenerational knowledge and friendship in our new (to us) neighborhood: a rare gift — at least in my world — people holding on to a 6-generation understanding of a place. He said he appreciated it too and also loves that he got to be alive in the 1960s: the last decade that our country had fully functional small towns where everybody made something, fixed something, shared something, and we weren't dependent on big distant corporations and Dairy Queen back then.

My neighbor said that at his age he's come to value the tribe here. What our political differences happen to be, matter far less now. What *any* of our divisive differences are matter far less now. You become more curious, he said: What is this tribe here about? And what am I in this tribe? When you're my age, he said.

And my age, I thought, perhaps presumptuously, given that I wasn't alive in the 1960s.

I mentioned that my parents just picked a town because it's close to us, though thousands of miles from their heritage home. Plus there are three credit unions to choose from, which makes bank-hating Dad happy, and a Subway sandwich shop, which makes Mom, who has Alzheimer's disease, happy. There she still knows the menu, ingredients, and the process plus she loves their raspberry white chocolate chip cookies. It's one of the few restaurants left on earth in which she can relax and enjoy life. The neighborhood they picked has independent living cottages + assisted living + memory care: the trifecta of awesomeness from their new perspective that *and* there's a Walmart just down the hill from their new place so they can easily do one-stop shopping and pick up their prescriptions.

Lately I've been dropping the need to be sad or worried or mad about Mom and Dad's very different selves and priorities now. Together we're fine most days. Beyond fine. I've also been dropping my own need to hate Subway and Walmart: not that I'm typically a patron of either when Mom and Dad aren't around (my ridiculous ego would deeply like you to know).

Frankly, I'm in awe at the glorious simplicity of their lives now.

Where:

> small loving family + supportive neighborhood
> + nearby credit union + Subway + Walmart
> = pure contentment and peace

And I've been shifting into the growing simplicity of my own life.

Where:

> the universe giggles while a progressive, Walmart-hating daughter
> openly admits Walmart's place
> in her own beloved parents'
> current happiness

The world is not as simple as we would like it to be.

Then again,
it is simple here walking
talking with neighbors.

The Voice of Unease

One day I will hear the voice of unease
before her tears fall.

I will take her small hand, slow down,
allowing the ample time she demands
to reacquaint us with this lucky life.

And when I do,
we will see a neighbor
teaching her dog how to dance.

We will notice nervous new bird parents
racing to feed their crying baby.

We will shut our eyes
pull the warm wind
into our souls.

I will stay with her until we relax,
breathe deeply:
until we both stubbornly insist on being the we
that we prefer to be.

Needed to Breathe Deeply Right Now: Choose 1

blank page
empty space
a face turning into wind

solitude
bare feet
a fuck-it attitude

a friend's voice
removing my head from my own behind, again

felt freedom to mess up
keep learning

felt connection to the universe herself

nature before me
shifting from particle to wave

well-filled lungs
music

closed eyes
open eyes

receiving help from everything

sitting on the earth
walking
swimming

a good belly scream

true community

watching a silly cat video
aka, leaving an offering to the Internet gods

sobriety

levity

whispering yes and no repeatedly

expanding into frivolity

We Are Not Strangers

My Grandma Del passed away last week. It was the day before my 43rd birthday, and about 2 months before her 88th birthday.

She was the last of my living grandparents. When Daniel called me to break the news to me, he woke me up, and the first thought that flickered across my just-waking mind was "Oh my God, I'm an orphan." This made me smile later, through my sadness.

My sister Jen and I immediately flew back to South Dakota and drove 2½ hours into the northeast corner of the state where we joined our family to mourn and celebrate her life.

In the past 10 years I've lost my two other grandparents, Daniel's grandparents, several friends, and several dogs and cats who were family too. I'm no longer the stranger to death that I was when my grandpa passed away 10 years ago. This time it felt like I was holding hands with my sadness, which meant that this time, in most moments, I could still receive the gifts of the present.

For example, this time I could notice how much good was still all around us.

I was conscious and curious about how previous versions of our family, and me, moved through difficult and sad times and how the right-now-us, and me, were moving through this one.

It felt like I was moving through my individual sadness and into gratitude for family and warm memories more easily and quickly this time.

I felt a tiny bit more present in the moment to comfort others and a teeny bit less like I was drowning in my own sadness this time.

I felt more comfortable saying goodbye at the viewing and crying with my entire family around me. I now know what my tears are, and I am rightly proud of them, and of us, not ashamed.

I wasn't entirely comfortable, but I was more comfortable than before.

And I felt truly there, and truly blessed to be there.

Until the morning of the funeral.

When we arrived, the chapel was full of people I didn't know. Strangers to me, this rural town I visited often as a kid but now just once each summer as an adult. My parents, Jen, and I were led to a separate room where all the rest of our family was. We learned that the four of us would walk into the chapel following the casket, because my mom is the oldest of her six siblings. Learned that everyone else in the family would follow in behind us.

The thought of walking through that huge room of strangers, while vulnerable and crying, and not being able to see the rest of our family because they were behind us, terrified me.

I thought briefly of suggesting that we instead file in in order from tallest to shortest so that I could be at the end. Or alphabetically, so that I could at least be somewhere in the middle. Saying these things aloud didn't feel appropriate to the moment, but the humor of the thoughts did make me feel a little better.

As we walked into the chapel, for a few moments I was right. It felt awful to be following my beloved Grandma Del, in a casket, down a long aisle, and through a large room full of strangers. Too exposed. I felt abandoned, lonely, then angry. My judgmental self showed up momentarily with the thought "This was poorly planned." Ah, silly, silly girl.

Because then they began to sing. As we walked, heads down in silence, they sang *Amazing Grace* to us, around us, for us, and my whole world shifted.

I actually looked up at their faces. I even saw a few people that I knew. And in a couple of the strangers' faces, I saw more tears and I saw pain that appeared deep, in some cases at least as deep as my own. And just like that, I was back to grateful. Back to blessed.

This community — my grandmother's community — was completely surrounding our family with love. They were hugging us. Lifting us up. Demonstrating that we were more connected to each other, and to the entire town and surrounding area, than we'd remembered. Well, than I'd remembered anyway.

As a non-church goer, I don't actually remember a word of the service or which Bible verses were read or any of the sermon that followed. I just don't connect with words written thousands of years ago and with lectures and lessons from strangers on high.

During the service I mostly thought about all the flowers and plants sent by friends. I thought about putting the photo boards together with family the day before and about other fun things we've done as a family. Thought about my grandma's house and yard and garden and holidays and humor and strength. I touched hands and shoulders and passed tissues to crying relatives.

And then I shut my eyes and felt the hundred or so rural, mostly conservative, mostly religious, farmers and townsfolk, sitting behind us, feeling our pain and crying our tears with us.

I thought about how they'd been singing to comfort all of us, including West coast city-dwelling, progressive, liberal, non-church-going, me.

We humans are not strangers.

How had I forgotten that?

We are not strangers. I know this now.

After the service, I watched my mom, who has Alzheimer's disease, blossom into her old self before my stunned eyes. Surrounded by people she knew as a child, supported by those deepest early memories, she became chatty and even introduced me to several people by name. By name! On her own! I hadn't witnessed that in almost decade. I was struck silent in awe as I watched pre-disease Mom emerge, hosting and laughing, for a while. This place of deep sadness transformed itself into a holy temple of gratitude. And I was there to feel it!

As we moved out into the warm wind and June sunshine of the beautiful old Lily Cemetery, my broken heart found peace.

Grandma Del's community, thank you for the reminder I needed at the exact moment I needed it. You will not, cannot, be strangers to me again. No matter what happens.

Rest in peace, Grandma Del. We love you.

What Does It Take to Create and Sustain Terabithia?

One of my favorite books as a kid was Bridge to Terabithia, a story of two young friends who overcome their troubled lives to create their own magical kingdom — called Terabithia — in the woods behind their homes. As I recall, the story is 80% friendship, magic, and wonder and 20% struggle, isolation, loss, and extreme sadness, especially near the end, because [spoiler alert] one of the two drowns. The story ends with the devastated friend creating a memorial to his fallen friend, getting the chance to help someone else in the way that she had helped him, and deciding to invite that new person into Terabithia. He was so changed by their friendship that he couldn't go back to the old self he knew, because the old him was gone.

As a kid, the struggle, isolation, loss, and extreme sadness parts of the story were sad, and yet they also made me feel honored — honored that a grownup author would so trust me to be ok with these parts of life too. Most of my experience of adults was of being shielded and protected from the loss and sadness parts of life. This story was new. This was an adult sharing more of the whole of life with me. I was part of something vaster than I'd imagined, and I was honored by the inclusion, the invitation into this world. My world.

Beyond feeling honored, the parts of the story that stayed in my memory as time passed were the parts I knew best as a child: friendship, magic, and wonder.

As kids, we were experts at these things. We had magic places like these everywhere. As a kid you couldn't throw a rock in my neighborhood without hitting a Terabithia-like place. Magic places that adults simply couldn't see: some tiny, some vast, some physical locations, and others entirely within our imaginations.

Every willow tree was, by its nature, a fort. Once we were inside, grownups literally couldn't see us.

One neighbor had a tree house with a rope ladder we could pull up to keep the little kids out.

We raced across a corn field to the crumbling, moss-covered foundation of a long-gone farm house in a stand of trees behind our edge-of-the-city neighborhood.

We performed last-rites ceremonies at the mouse, bird, hamster, and bug cemetery in another stand of trees near my friend Amy's house.

We visited a very old man—whose name I never knew but who listened to our adventures and shared his bananas with us — who lived in the basement apartment next door to my friend Lori's house.

When I was 10, inspired by the book, my friend Kristi and I actually made our own Terabithia in the trees beside her grandma's house. We spent a lot of time building it, decorating it, eating in it, and guarding it from dragons (mostly her little brother and my little sister, sorry guys) and only abandoned it when the South Dakota winter snows made all its lovely carpet remnants smell really bad.

We knew how to create and sustain Terabithias as children. We found them within ourselves and let them go—with just a touch of sadness—to move on to new ones.

Until this summer, I hadn't consciously thought about the Bridge to Terabithia story for years. Then Tabitha showed up — bringing fun craft projects into our home/neighborhood coworking space, and I said to her "You're making our home feel like Terabithia!" The word just showed up like an old friend, as did Tabitha.

Now, almost everywhere I go, almost everywhere I look, I see Terabithia. My own world.

The people who come into our free community coworking space are all pirates, playmates, friends, and neighbors now.

I see Terabithia in our drinks on the front porch, board game playing, movie nights, potlucks, BBQs, and pumpkin carving. In backyard bartering and cider pressing and festivals and dessert buffets. In connecting via Facebook, under the covers at midnight, to commiserate when we get scared. In Chris' face when he gets excited or frustrated by a new game. I see it even in the online links friends send me: in artwork and music and theater and dance and poetry and humor. Fisher recently sent me to see what the word Koinonia means and learn about its history. It's pretty cool. You should look it up.

I find Terabithia in the tragedy and the sad stories too. Terabithia is there, too.

I see Terabithia in the spaces around us.

At home, it's everywhere. In my deep love of found objects: rocks, shells, driftwood, seeds, and sticks.

In our practical love of old, well-made, inexpensive things: the $5 chairs I got at UWSurplus, a library of worn second-hand books, Daniel's old cameras that have become works of art, Narisa's flea market finds. I see it in our love of things made by friends and solidly made things that will out-live us: like the 500-year table that now sits in the dining room, the joyfully painted rocks on top of it, and in the artwork on our walls created by artist and photographer friends and by us ourselves.

I see Terabithia now, too, in all the places to sit and dream and read and play in our home, in our yard, and in our neighborhood. In the cozy chairs. Rogue benches.

In the empty lots where we throw wildflower seed balls and then anxiously wait for spring to see if flowers come up. In large rocks I can sit on. In the neighborhood pub that still has my 10-year-old-self's go-to video game Qubert. In the little bike shop, and little movie theater, and little radio station, and coffee shops, and Earl's barber shop where community is fed and thrives.

In the little orchid-like flowers on our rosemary plant (baby rosemary orchids!!).

And I also see an evolution in myself — a front garden designed to bring neighbors closer, not to keep dragons out. A front door held open wide, most days.

What does it take to create and sustain Terabithia?

It's not the difficult, complicated, impossible task most adults think it is. Doesn't take tons of time and money and outside experts and consultants and degrees. It doesn't require utter seriousness, laser focus, group consensus, perfect connections, extreme efficiency, extra smart people, people agreeing on stuff, or a gap-free resume. Bleh.

Total bullshit, my friends. Lies.

Do not believe the grownups. They know not what they do.

I decided recently that getting a case of the grownups is far worse than getting the mumps or chicken pox or measles. Because for many, the grownups is the death of magic, wonder, and even friendship, and the stupid thing can last for decades! Eeew. But I digress...

I create and sustain Terabithia.

I do.

"an entire ocean, in single drop" (thanks Rumi) me

No resources — of any sort — that I don't already have within me and around me are required. Cast out those grownup demons.

Kid you can look at a tree and see a fort, can look at an empty lot and see a playground, can create time to slow down and speak thoughtful farewell words over the body of a dead insect, and share a banana and a story with someone feeling lonely.

If you have kid you, then you already have Terabithia.

It's in your pocket right now.

Go ahead.

Look.

3. Fire, Peace, Courage

I Break My Heart Each Morning

I break my heart each morning
so there is room for her

her memory and story
her history inside of me

disease that slowly separates
her away from her

beyond disease
a slow release
of precious self to daughters

Mom
we break ourselves each morning
let our hearts be wounds
now find those hearts
a gentle gauze
wound around the world

Hearth Fire

Mom
I love the way you love
warm folding of laundry
soft fuzzy robes
drying dishes, the game of where
to put them
you rubbing my hands and feet
always present for me
here beyond memory

so let synapses misfire
let brains tinder the fire of smiling hearts

I thought Alzheimer's was a fire burning away at us
until a predilection to leave the essential untouched
became infinitely obvious
burning away instead the noisy distance
that too-busy charade
our frustration, guilt, shame, regret, fear, anger, contempt
even sorrow
mine yours ours
until they fade into background:
dust bunnies, ember elves
shadow puppets
former selves

I was so then
so blind
Alzheimer's is not a flame to burn us

We are the flame

We are the flame

we release demons
set them in boats
kick their sterns and cut their ropes

we set then adrift
here in the now

you become hearth fire
I become sky

at ease within all dis-ease

just us again
like always

giggling above the laundry

Family Drift

1. The Question

Why do you feel the need to make the rift in our family all about your mom's disease? You know too well that's not the case at all.

Damn good question.

Thanks for asking.

2. The Life Raft

for 35 years I experienced our family as 98% love
2% occasional mild grouchiness
nobody's perfect, yet
you guys are to me

for the next 9 years, every day
I listened, watched, did battle
as Alzheimer's hacked away at Mom and Dad
both
I learned to accept powerlessness against it
that everything we've tried to help, will ever try, is shit
window dressing
arranging knickknacks, dusting bookshelves on the Titanic

Alzheimer's choked me, left me sobbing, sunk me, tried to drown me
burned me more times than I can count
it burned me bare
I'm burning still and here I am
the essential intact, still grateful
Alzheimer's released the voice and the artist and the mother
and the father in my sister and me
restored the mermaids

instead of drowning us it is releasing us from fear

to become an entire ocean
returning more of our parents to us than we've ever known before
returning more of our planet to us than we could possibly
have received before

as ocean, we can reimagine anything, even Alzheimer's, as a Life Raft

as ocean, we've pushed away those who hurt us
we accept that we've pushed you away, we don't blame you

as ocean, we've pulled toward us those who forgive and love us
flaws and all
we've pulled some relatives closer, wrapping them around us
warm blankets and fuzzy socks on bitter nights
we accept your anger at abandonment as our own

So, livid cousin, devastated aunt,
ghost uncles on whose behalf wicked-brave women speak to me
I am sorry for your pain and my part in it
I am sorry when you feel poetry as a cleaver in my hand
or weight around your neck
I am sorry when you experience me as a basher of family

that is not my intent
and I honor what you feel
I'll call myself a liar before I ever call you one

So why do I imagine Alzheimer's as a Life Raft now?

to hang on to you

as long as Alzheimer's holds its share of the blame
for this extended family rift —
holds my perspective too —
I don't have to lose you.

I don't have to lose you.

You.

You.

Maybe I have to lose you for a little while, while we heal the rifts within, but not forever.

Look again. At us. At what we're saying. At who we are.
Where we are.

You will always be within my we. This we...

We are not exiled. We are not silent. We are not helpless. We are not liars. We are not orphans. We are not bashers of family. We have not been cut in half. None of us. That's our fear talking. Our fear. We are family.

We are poets and pilots.

We are parents and gardeners and farmers.

We are mermaids in matching pajamas.

We are the whole bloody ocean now.

When deeply wounded we can be cleavers.
We're both more vulnerable and more powerful than ever.

Nobody's perfect, yet
you guys are to me

3. Stupid Cleaver, You Missed Our Hearts Again

Alzheimer's disease
you meat cleaver
you hacker of brain and bone
you forest fire turning memory and limbs to ash
you can't get at these hearts

Alzheimer's disease you tried to exile us:
I struggle to understand how any of this is the family's fault.
(So do I. You are still my family. Hope I'm still yours.)

Alzheimer's disease you tried to accuse us:
*When you write about our family and how many walked away, you know
that's not true.*
(I walked away. Several of us did. We had to heal. We were bleeding.
This is true for us. You are still our family. Hope we're still yours.)

Alzheimer's disease you tried to orphan and silence us:
*Writing about family that chose to distance themselves. No one chose that.
Everyone is reading it and in awe of the bashing.*
(I chose distance to repair and rebuild my broken heart. So did my
sister. Are we no one to you now? How is it that you still hear us and
we still hear you?)

Alzheimer's disease you tried to hack us clean in half:
Your writing is warm and loving. Hang on tight to those Berg *traits.*
(Those are Kane traits, too. I cannot be divided. I can't divide myself.
Not even when people I love ask me to. Alzheimer's taught me that.
And you taught me that, family.)

Alzheimer's disease you hack out my eyes, blinding me, my ears, deaf-
ening me, but somehow you keep missing my heart entirely:
*Had lawyers and judges not been introduced to our family none of this
would have happened and you know it. My God you make us seem like
heartless people who abandoned you and that hurts more than anything.
Her siblings would give anything to see her again and you've chosen to
blog about what a bunch of assholes we are. When it all really comes
down to that fucking court case.*
(Yes. For you it comes down to that. My heart expanded to hold
your truth when I allowed it to fully break. Yet even on the days you
rage at me for being me, your love is still there. My broken heart sees
yours. I am the last human on earth who would ever call you heartless. So put that in your pipe and smoke it, ragey. I'm so sad for our
pain and loss that sometimes I have to step away to mend. But not
today. Today I welcome your pain and rage. I envelop it. I am pain
and rage now. Pain is my guide. Rage is my bitch. So bring it. All of
it. I will withstand your pain and your rage. I will hug you tighter for

them when I next see you. I expect you'll do the same. We are not made of such fragile stuff as we imagine, you and I.)

Alzheimer's disease you turned me into a writer of sad and dreary form letters:

Dear [insert another family member who I love here], *I'm disconnecting from you for a year. I hope we can reconnect again later on. I learned today that the poem I wrote yesterday devastated you. I am sorry about that, it wasn't my intent. I am angry about a disease, and my own powerlessness in the face of it to stop it from destroying my parents. Rage is part of that. Rage is part of me now. This is me now. But blame isn't. I'm not angry at you guys. I don't hate you. I don't blame my family. I love you. For my own health, and my sister's, I need to write about our experience of Alzheimer's disease. Disconnecting temporarily allows me to do that without inadvertently hurting you again. If you need me for anything urgent this year, you can reach me at _____. I look forward to reconnecting again in the future. I love you. — Lori*

Alzheimer's disease, you fucking jerk
you made me the cleaver
there goes another of my precious limbs

4. Four Deep Breaths

5. Ocean

as your arms tire
day by day
release into me
drop cleavers in
sink blood-weary hands ever deeper
I have all the time in the world

I am ocean
we are mermaids
no leg to stand on among us

beyond words
beyond loss
beyond exile
beyond welcome

the essential
holds
our family
holds
us

those who cried this ocean with me
aren't anchors

you are my life raft

this we
here now
is my way home

Hate within Me Has a 3-Minute Shelf Life

We thought the Alzheimer's diagnosis would be hard.
Then, that the slow losing of Mom as we knew her
would be beyond hard.
These things seemed shatteringly difficult for so very many others.
How could we expect anything else?

But we're nine years in now.
Now we know.
Those aren't the hard parts.

I

Alzheimer's strips away what doesn't matter right now,
exposing what does matter, to anyone fully present,
again and again,
much like the best
within schooling, science, religion,
philosophy, nature, art, comedy, parenting,
and house cleaning.
Strips away what doesn't matter. Reveals what does.
First, within her, then within us,
then within those who love us enough to move with us.

Sure, some days we expect to shatter.
But we actually don't. We ripple.
Alzheimer's is a stone
thrown onto a pond
shaking us as it sinks deeper
but if we move together
we don't shatter.

We are better for it, most days,
if we shift, turn into it,
pay closer attention
accept help
adjust our individual, our collective, selves.

Alzheimer's first stripped away her filters
so she always says exactly what's on her mind.
Sometimes it's painful, yes, and
sometimes it's fun, even hilarious.

Then it stripped away her boundaries,
so she greets and loves whomever she wants to now, even strangers.
Turns on her heel, walking away from those she doesn't like,
without fuss, regret, or guilt.
It strips away our boundaries too.
We, too, now greet and love those we're meant to.
Walk, without guilt/regret/fuss, just like her,
away from situations that regularly cause us pain.

Then it stripped away independence:
hers, Dad's, ours, our closest others'
exposing our interdependence.
Good riddance extreme independence.
You are the most twisted, overrated value our country cranks out.
We are stronger now. More honest with ourselves, each other.
Explore depths across ourselves
we couldn't reach before.
The closer we get, the stronger we get,
the more truly independent we are.

Last year it washed away her fear of looking bad
exposing silliness and love and laughter at her core. Yes, and
that's rippling out into us now
for example, writer me becoming poet me,
my sister becoming a mother herself,
as our now-ridiculous fears wash out to sea with hers.

It strips away the illusion of control
requiring and allowing us
to prioritize ourselves
to create and re-create together
at times by the minute
a new response to this right now.

We're becoming improvisation masters,
just like her. She's our muse. Our center.
Like she's always been
always can be.

This year it's striping away the years
giving us a front row seat
to a gathering of people
we never imagined we'd meet.
To a mom at times in her forties, thirties, twenties
her teens
grade school
preschool.
This, because we're together, in itself, is not that hard.
Mom, at all stages, was, is
Happy. Loving. Curious. Helpful. Silly. Most of the time.
Cranky only when tired, and often not even then.
This is where the deeper blessings of our family reveal themselves.
Not all Alzheimer's families are this lucky.
Mom is happy, back then and right now, one, and the same.
And even luckier, on her darkest days, she still taps into empathy,
using it as a life line, sometimes better than the rest of us.
We are so so so amazingly lucky.
Good to remember when we find ourselves embarrassed
by her embrace of total strangers.

As we watch the stone
send ripples out across the pond,
it's quickly revealed
who our closest friends and family are:
who moves closer, with us, who moves farther away,
or is pushed away.
Those who move with us love all of us, no matter what,
are deep wellsprings of empathy,
bring out the best in us when we are at our worst,
have the courage to assume the best,
the ability lead with forgiveness and kindness no matter what.

What a tremendous gift in the face of fog and chaos:
to know exactly who your partners in crime are today, and who aren't
to find solace, peace, even here
in the wake of departing loved ones.

II

For us, what's hard about Alzheimer's isn't Alzheimer's.

What's hard is some people's response to it. For example:

1. Well-intentioned friends who show up to fix us,
instead of just being present, with us, here, open, hanging out,
improvising with us.
Yes, and hello,
that was me until Alzheimer's disease.

2. People who don't understand the disease's insidious impacts
to primary caregivers
who take bizarre new behavior, like silence or short-temperedness,
personally
who hate Dad for it.
We are sorry. And we are selective now about who we see
because we have to be or we'll shatter.
Hate him/us and you're out, for now.
Thanks to Alzheimer's we know this means *just for now*.
We hope you do to. We mean no offense.

3. Ourselves some days.
Sometimes we wallow in individual pain.
Forget the feelings of others.
We have to forgive ourselves more often now.
We grow weary. Make big mistakes.
We are becoming masters of forgiveness
because we have to be.
No choice.
To ripple not shatter,
we then open to growing closeness
because of shared pain

instead of chronically dwelling
on individual pain.
Otherwise we get stretched too thin
forget improvisation, how to love without limit.

4. A father/caregiver/husband
trying to do everything himself.
Fucking Greatest Generation
how I want to smack the lot of you some days.
Refusing to ask for or allow more caregiving help
for years.
Exhausting himself into a shell of his former self.
Living with his own chronic sicknesses.
Needlessly.
Doing way too much.
Needlessly.
Bringing forth his own sleeplessness, memory loss and confusion
bringing forth new stories of family pain as a result.
Reimagining extended family to highlight anger, erase love,
at times seeing monsters where nothing more than
frightened people exist
at times creating monsters
tilting at windmills preferable to receiving help.
And, far, far worse, that an exhausted man
manages to pull forth bad behavior from trusted others. Horrible.
I still can't believe he has that much influence in him.
Will he join us in rippling across the water?
Or will he shatter?
Too close to call.

5. People who try to mentally divide
our entirely undividable parents
trying to love and support
one half,
raising one up as a saint while insisting
the other is the devil incarnate.
Sorry, folks, there is no half here. We are whole.

Team Linda has become Team Jinda now.
All good. All crazy. All the time.
As are we,
with anyone brave enough
to stand with crazy-now us.
They are so whole, in fact,
that at times I wonder if it will be easier for him to join her there –
walk into the lonely chaotic fog of memory-loss land –
than to watch her go there alone.

6. Distant, angry, attacking people anywhere
who judge from far away,
assume the worst of people instead of circumstances,
without firsthand understanding,
content to assume, blame, point fingers from afar,
instead of moving closer and connecting.
So goodbye politicians. Goodbye Internet trolls.
Goodbye chronic haters.
We literally don't have the time.
Yes, and
wow, that used to be me
content to stew and hate from a distance
before Alzheimer's.

Hate within me now has a 3-minute shelf life.

7. People who blame the primary caregiver
for "taking her away from us."
Please, for the love of God,
knock that shit off.
As if people who love her
could really be stopped
from seeing her, calling them, writing her,
visiting, sending care packages,
communicating with her somehow.

We communicate more now than ever before,
even though most days,

she has very few words to work with.
They love visits, letters, cards, packages.
She needs a sidekick now
to stay on track
finish sentences and thoughts,
in person, on speakerphone, or Skype,
but she loves conversation (before 5 p.m.)
loves listening. Loves presence. Loves you.

I know it's scary. Seems impossible.
But it's not actually impossible for you, like it is for them.
You still have the gifts of time and letter writing,
of sending cards, little packages covered with doodles, or stickers.
Of having free time
being able to pick up a phone,
remember and dial numbers,
to reach out to someone you love. Of learning Skype
so you can see someone at a distance. Emailing.

Stop. Blaming. Others.
for your perfectly reasonable and acceptable decision
to step away for a while from
what you can't bear to see and hear right now.
A sleeping-half-the-day,
sick-all-the-time, shaky,
barely-holding-it-together,
74-year-old man
can be a major pain in the ass
but he is not the obstacle you imagine him to be.
Our own fear is.
Our own apparent inability
to do anything at all to kick Alzheimer's to the curb.
Our own inability
to change what IS into what WAS.

Dad's in no position anymore to bat away hands outstretched in love.
But we are in a position to love

even in the face of anger and rage at being lonely,
destined to fail to save the love of your life,
at having to grieve every damn day.
For 15 years (no wait, 5 left now, if we're lucky).
WE are not powerless now. Just the opposite.
We are being asked to become stronger and more powerful
than we were.
Accept what is. Channel anger into something good.
Step out in courage! Be more persistent!
More fucking loving than ever before!
She would for us if she could.
And you may never believe us now, but, if he could:
So. Would. He.
You may never forget that you turned your back on them in return.
I really don't want that for you. We love you.

8. And to the family member
content to periodically yell
at my pregnant sister
for not adequately fixing
our evil father
while she's working with him to feed Mom, dress Mom, bathe Mom,
noticing his closed, tired eyes,
hands shaking from his own non-stop coughing,
from forgetting to eat.
Watching him fall asleep mid-sentence, mid-joke, mid-conversation,
because he's been awake every hour, all night again, with Mom.
Watching Mom bring him his pills, with water,
because he only has the energy
to help her remember to always take *hers* regularly
at times forgetting his own.

STOP venting at my sister.

Bring your anger your pain your frustration
your deepest rage
to me now.

I will hear you for her.
She needs a break.
Honor this request
or you might step on her heart so completely that you'll lose her.
Completely.
I doubt you will. But I'd rather not take that risk
with her heart or yours.

III

Alzheimer's never asks us what we want. Doesn't give us a choice.
Not those of us really close to her.
Here in the heart of it
we must get closer to people who want to connect and help,
drop pretense,
reveal vulnerabilities,
move through pain together.
We must get on with the business of loving who we love
letting go of people and things and places
we don't have the energy for right now.
When we don't, we shatter.

We shatter.

She gives us no choice.

FUCK THIS DISEASE! FUCK THAT WE REGULARLY LOSE
PEOPLE — A FUCKING LOT OF PEOPLE FROM OUR LIVES
IT TURNS OUT — BECAUSE OF IT!
FUCK THAT FAILURE TO SAVE MOM IS OUR ONLY
CERTAINTY! FUCK THAT WE FAILED TO KEEP OUR
EXTENDED FAMILY TOGETHER THROUGH THIS!
FUCK EARLY ONSET ALZHEIMER'S THAT GIVES JEN AND
I CONSTANT DAILY REMINDERS THAT WE MAY GET
THIS DISEASE AND PUT OUR HUSBANDS AND LOVED
ONES THROUGH FUCKING ALL OF THIS AGAIN IN A FEW
YEARS! FUCK FUCK FUCK!*

*Hmm, I may be more at risk for Tourette's than Alzheimer's. ;-)

IV

Ok, so we shatter
we fall completely apart
yes, and
here we are
still ripples in the same pond.
We're still us.
Still the pond.

You don't scare me now, shatter, you ratty little weasel.

Bring it.

Because

Wow are we learning how to love right now, flaws and all.
Flaws are where we connect. We love flaws!

Wow are we deeply grateful for tiny little things,
the smallest kindnesses.
That sunshine against your cheek? A gift.

Wow can we move fluidly, together, with exquisite grace. Laughing.
Without words. Like geese and jazz musicians.

Wow can we get through anything, forgive anything,
including ourselves.

What?! We can now control how long hate stays within us?
Aware that it is our choice and that this too-short life is precious?

We can choose seconds or minutes with hate and not be stuck with it
for months or years? We can save our energy/selves/family/love/world
from you?

I had no idea we were this powerful.

I choose 3 minutes with hate now, out of habit. Take that, silly hate,
stupid shatter.

What?! We can have fun now: the deepest fun we've ever had

Any where? Any time?

We can walk up to anyone?! Hug, with true connection, whomever we want to hug?!

Good God. The whole earth is our playground.

I find myself happy to be Alzheimer's student.

I find myself happy to be her student, most days.**
**See previous FUCK FUCK FUCK!

I'm happy to spend time in her company
among others here
people who are willing to move into exhaustion and anger
and rage visibly
who come back out again, this time holding hands and smiling.

Our rag-tag Alzheimer's improv troupe
is learning that the way to keep things moving
is to respond with "Yes! And…"
to what IS right now
to the worlds created by our companions,
whether or not we understand or agree
or think their world has any ground or truth
in our reality.

We're learning to expand their world and ours,
by weaving our worlds together in real time
co-creating new worlds within which all of our perspectives
and responses
are valid, proper, and true.

Today – more than 10 years into Alzheimer's – Mom is a master of world weaving.
The Dalai Lama of improv.
While the rest of us just try to keep up.

It can be frustrating to encounter people who can't really see us now, can't improvise with us right now,

especially loved ones we used to count on.
But except for being tired and scared at times, ourselves,
we have no reason to bear anyone ill will
not anymore.

If we step away from you
we're just not ready right now
to have our world expanded by yours.
Or you're not quite ready to see us
as we truly are
right now.

V

We have become a river.

We aren't what we used to be.

Some people fear us now. We live with that.

Some love us more than ever: closer and reminded
that we're still us, still here
loving to laugh, cry, and hang out.

Belting out *Sisters* from White Christmas sillier and sexier than ever.

Inventing brand new music as we go.

You just have to be willing to see more of us now
willing to say "Yes! And…"
willing to believe that you, too,
if you step toward us
will survive the chaos, survive the shatter
to come out playing together
on the other side.

Winter's Orphans Springtime's Clowns

I

with tears,
cloaked in half-truths
clinging to vague, unexamined fear and rage
the adults turned
scattered to earth's farthest corners
from great distance
built walls
weapons
did battle.

Fucking grownups.

II

Left behind on wide open plains
Winter's abandoned children faced hard choices
no choice, really

stay
face
more-whole truths
broken hearts everywhere
loss
anger on all sides
fear everywhere
the worst within

hold on
to fun
laughter

honor
lightness of spirit
darkness of origin

create
impossible new old selves
disinclined to hide

glide down, through, then off of hatred
hands up in the air
like a slide

sit with the
weeping
stay with abandoned
selves
cry with the
wounded
cradle the
dying
embrace the
dead

accept the cracks

accept abandonment

accept the rage that moves through you

accept this new state of orphanhood, this too-soon adulthood
like you watched your cousins do
once before
rising from ashes
more amazing than ever
beautiful, wise, kinder, gentler, made strong
on winter's harsh plane

III

With grownups fled
your first instincts were to rush to fix things,
build walls out of hatred, and/or
run away.
To look away, sequester yourself, like the adults did.

But utterly surrounded by orphans,
new options arrived
new voices
the trees, the stars, all the dead
whisper

Not yet child. Be still.
First relax, be held.
Be held by your own arms: now your own mother/father.
Be held by the family that remains:
mother universe, father time, mother nature, other orphans.
Stay with it. Name it. Don't rush.
Grieve. Rage. Mourn. Collapse.
Give in to the urge to play when you're ready.
Play as if Life herself depended on it.
Be amazed: they are enough
More amazed: you are enough

gather internal strength this winter
look deeper
until you find slivers of uncertainty within certainty
greater truths around untruths
seeds for doing better:
vulnerability
lightly held connection
shared pain
humor

a secret love of winter, even as we curse it, shovel it
friendship

jump up and down in anger
until you remember, feel
the pure joy in jumping
up
and down

notice
how you yourself moved your anger through you
in through your head
out your now-warm feet

IV

with almost invisible seeds
they themselves can't clearly see
Winter's badass children will rebuild themselves until they're laughing
until we're all laughing

who better to start a sacred choir of laughter
than Winter's abandoned children
united as friends
content with who they are
held within loss
jumping up and down
kickstarting lost humanity
powered from within?

V

we are Winter's badass orphans

abandoned
we break
rage
mourn
play
start over
with broken, lost selves
raw
bare and unhidden
vulnerable
yet remarkably held

adults may never understand our silly
they forgot the power of silly
yet couldn't fully pull content from within discontent
or find mystery and wonder within ruin
without it

Bitches, we can.

We can Scooby Fucking Doo this.

VI

walls we once cursed, like our parents,
we taught ourselves to cherish
those walls meant becoming our own elders
forming more open, silly, bleeding hearts within ourselves
broken hearts, perfect, for turning walls into playgrounds

the same walls that made enemies of our too distant parents
are making
better parents
better community members

better leaders
crafters, builders, farmers
artists, poets
and elders
right now
of us all

watch us demonstrate

VII

Dear, dear, fucking grownups
Good God it's hard to love you some days

but we do
we love you
we honor you
by making different choices than you did

happy humans don't appear magically come springtime
not yet they don't
peace for us means slowing down together
crafting new selves
from raw red earth, rubble, spit, and bubble gum
right now
we know we need every unique perspective
every person
to survive, thrive

You forgot that your own children are abandoned behind your walls.
Orphaning you within.

Welcome to our world, orphan.
Running away is not an option here.
Walls and distance and distraction don't work here.
Here we face the music together, awkwardly re-learn to dance,
or we die trying.

The empty world you left us is cold, shattered.
Walls in all directions we turn.
Can't you hear us screaming outside your fortresses?
Open your eyes. We're not monsters, dear hearts.
We're all just abandoned children.
We will see this for you if you can't through your self-blinded eyes.

VIII

We pulled ourselves through the harshest winter
together
hand in hand
with those we love

those you failed to teach us to hate

we have become our own elders

your generation will be the last to die
trying to heal across great distances
behind walls, blind,
stuck, drowning in smelly, stagnant rage

ours will be the last one abandoned
to die alone in the street

this shit stops with us

IX

our children
will watch us work with neighbors
to tear down old walls
build parks

our children
will help us plant vegetables
in abandoned lots

fruit on rooftops
herbs in pots

our children
will hear us creating art, laughing
with those we were taught to hate

our children
will grow up laughing and crying together
unafraid
to bring their fears out in the open
in rubble-magic playgrounds
emerging as springtime's clowns

Until this rings true for all our children
this rings hollow for all our children.

This is our truth. We own it. We don't look away.
We are offering our lives — Gens X, Y, Z — to bring this through.

X

Welcome the clowns.

Weaving wounds together
with
love and humor
stayed-with grief
moar gratitude
soft twinkles in their eyes

gentle curious flexible fingers and souls
finding and using wordless threads — goose bumps, belly laughs,
cheek-tears, skipping, pee-inducing giggles, and awe —
pulling wounded worlds back together

bowing deeper silly bows

mourning wide open, visible and exposed

allowing the dead

finally honored

to go

Through the Flames, Watch for Deep Grace

Turning away from the deepest suffering means turning away from the deepest grace. That's the heart of this essay.

Several friends and I have asked ourselves the same question this past year:

> How do I keep an open heart
> while standing in the depths
> of pain, of suffering, of hell?

Everybody's answer is slightly different.

As a new poet, my answer has been to surround myself with other poets and writers who've done the same. This year especially, as my family and I fell into our own personal mini-hell, I've turned to black poets, black writers, and other voices that stay with extraordinary pain, creating through it, pulling forth stunning creation and broken-open, stunning, badass new selves. Work that other broken-hearted, angry, and frightened people can stay with and feel. Or willingly return to, when they're stronger. Broken, weeping people, like me.

The voices of black poets, especially, have pushed me along this year when I thought the pain of my family would shatter me. They surrounded me when it did shatter me. They celebrated with me when I came out the other side a new creature: stronger, gentler, fiercer, kinder, beautiful: a voice forged in fire.

Staying with pain, standing in the fire, in your own hell, is horrible. It is horrific. Words fail. There is screaming and yelling and crying and rage and grieving and mourning and exhaustion and not getting out of bed and cowering and hiding and giving up entirely. The only true words that can emerge at this point are: "This is hell. I am in hell."

I've learned to listen to voices that have lived through and spoken those words. And to those who've died and had others speak those words on their behalf. They were my saviors this year in many ways.

It can take a long time to get to these words. Yet, once spoken, the words "This is hell." can bring forth a new self. One cracked open to and receiving deeper insight, growth, clarity, strength, peace, friendship, and grace. Ridiculously deep grace. Grace that pre-hellfire you couldn't even imagine.

Suffering is horrible. You have to let it be what it is: horrible. Name it. Face it. Fall apart.

Then, not before, you can become more graceful. Falling apart is important. It allows suffering to move through you instead of pooling and stagnating within you. Suffering can become a tremendous gift when we're ready. A tremendous gift to a community or a country when we're ready.

We're ready.

In Ferguson. At the center of this United States in November in 2014. At the center of our collective, unspoken, ignored, stagnating and sinking-us hell.

To my ear, saying that black lives matter is not saying that the lives of law enforcement officers don't matter. It's the opposite. It's a reminder to those of us still avoiding our pain to wake up, see the fire we're all standing in, and remember that black lives matter. Remember that black children's lives matter. That watching black children die in the street, and anywhere else, has been breaking our collective heart again and again and again in this country for a long time now. That killing hurts everyone. Much of white America is ready to listen now. The repeated, pointless, death of person after person after person in this country has pulled us into our own hell. All of us. This searing pain and fear and anger when another person is killed for holding cigarettes or toys or candy, or walking or driving down the wrong street, or just looking at somebody the wrong way? And they're killed for it?!

This is what hell feels like.

To my ear, which now contains my heart, people saying *black lives matter* are saying this:

This is hell. I am in hell. We are in hell. Talk to me. Work with me. Help in whatever way you can before our whole country burns to the ground on the backs of dead children.

Hard to hear. Hard to say. Hard to write.

And not everyone is ready to hear and say these words, even now.

But I am.

I've been through my own hell this year, and I find that it's much easier to listen now, to face hell, and to speak. I don't have to turn away from suffering to find grace. Grace is always here.

I can stand with those in hell right now. #BlackLivesMatter

When I take that stand, I can bear the loss of friends who cannot bear to even look at where I'm standing right now. I can take their anger, fear, rage, and disgust. And I can receive them as friends whenever they choose to return.

I can stand with the vulnerable. With those who walk together, unarmed, terrified, with little hope, yet moving anyway, for the sake of their neighbors, children, family, and selves. People throwing their whole being/community/country onto the fire for everyone's sake, not just their own. Because they know we'll be better for it.

I can stand with those who have stood in the heart of their own hell, burned, shattered completely, and stepped forth new people, willing and able to speak for those who no longer have a voice.

Wow, do they move with grace.

There are hundreds of links available now to find and follow if you have the courage and space within you to do something in response to what you know is happening in Ferguson right now. My dear journalist friend shared this one — 12 Things White People Can Do Now Because Ferguson — specifically for those unaccustomed to stepping into the fire of racism and white supremacy at all, let alone together. Google it.

This essay is for people who can't do anything right now. People caught up in their own mini-hells, for example, too exhausted and sad and beaten down and scared to extend care out beyond the smallest of circles yet. I get it. I've been there. So recently that my tears aren't even dry yet.

I ask one small thing, for your own sake. If you cannot bear to act or look at Ferguson right now, please don't look entirely away. Instead, look for those in the heart of the fire who move with the deepest grace. They are there. Look closer or ask someone to look for you. Chaos will organize itself around them. Watch and notice that even chaos bows before deep grace. Everything else becomes background noise.

Watch for those moving with deep grace in the heart of hell. Watch and learn. They will teach you how to keep your heart open within the deepest suffering and pain. How to survive your own hell.

You need that deep grace now more than ever. We all do.

Don't look away.

Beauty Does Not Stay Down

before you mourn your mom smiling out from behind
the gauze of her disease,
remember

        beauty will not sit down

before you expect your dad to be reasonable, to let go of both Mom
and who he is this instant,
remember

        beauty will not sit down

before you ask your cousin, your self, to abandon rage
about grief and loss, remember

        beauty will not sit down

before you say goodbye to someone, certain your story ends here,
remember

        beauty will not sit down

before you expect someone to stop being so negative all the time,
remember

        beauty will not sit down

before you apologize for being yourself again, remember

        beauty will not sit down

before you concern yourself with their motives, with yours, remember

        beauty will not sit down

before you feel wounded by words spoken at the table, or online
words pouring forth from countless lifetimes of brethren in streets
gunned down, remember Mike Brown

        beauty will not sit down

before you look away in horror from girls bought and sold for sex and
pennies,
recall

          beauty will not stay down

before you accept what is said about you, about us, as the truth,
remember

          beauty will not stay down

before you decide you're not brave enough for this life
curl up, rest
recall the seed in the ground

          you will rise up again

          you will rise again

          you rise again

          you rise

          you

          !

beauty does not stay down

4. Sustained Creation

Noticing Miracles

Our pair of resident bald eagles have been away from home for a month — off on their annual river-fishing working vacation, we've heard from our other new neighbors — after their baby grew up and left the nest in August. I didn't realize how much I'd miss seeing the eagles every morning out the kitchen windows as I make tea. I miss them.

A few minutes ago, I heard an ominous buzz coming from our bedroom. A mean-looking wasp had flown in the open deck door and apparently trapped herself against the door glass trying to get back out. I sprung into action, herding the cats out of the room and then ushering her back outside with a magazine. She didn't protest: flew out and then straight up immediately.

As my eyes followed her ascent to make sure she was really gone, I saw one of the most amazing things I've ever seen. Way up in the sky, against sun-touched clouds, there were 40 bald eagles (I counted) slow dancing. As they circled and dipped together, it looked like a well-choreographed waltz: slow, relaxed, rhythmic. I've lived 23 years in the Pacific Northwest, and I've never seen anything like it. They waltzed and waltzed, slowly moving inland.

I felt that this is a group of Whidbey-based resident eagle pairs, like ours, returning from their river-fishing extended family vacations and saying goodbye here, on the corner of the island, before heading back to their homes scattered across the island. There may be other reasons for what they were doing, but I know what I saw. It was amazing. I would have missed it entirely if that mean-looking wasp hadn't decided to help a sister out.

I haven't been a church goer since I was a kid. Hierarchically organized religions aren't the right fit for me. But I believe in miracles.

There are reasons for what happens beyond human logic, thought, and beyond what anyone else says we should believe in.

Reasons that come to us from deep within, when we are annoyed, lifted off our feet by a buzzing wasp, only to find ourselves standing open-mouthed, alone, and awe-struck.

bearing witness to a sky full of slow dancing eagles

recognizing sisterhood with a wasp

feeling, moving, seeing with a more whole self

and only then

noticing

miracles

How to Greet a Seal like Eva

It's really foggy here today. I can see the end of the dock but not much else out there. The whole world looks like a down pillow from my window.

As Eva dog and I walked the beach this morning, a curious seal poked her head out of the water to watch us. Thanks to the fog and the tide, she was really close, perhaps just 30 feet away. The seal followed, popping up to see us every 15 seconds or so. Seals never get this close. In fact, in our first year here, Eva never noticed seals following us. Until today.

We were standing in the sand at the rounded, low-tide beach right at the point of Sandy Point. Looking back into the neighborhood, with the fog surrounding the brightly painted little homes, was like looking into a snow globe that we ourselves live in. Fog is cool.

Eva raced ahead, pretending to chase a rabbit while really looking for a stick for me to throw. I squatted down to look at the seal from her vantage point. I was impressed with myself for thinking of this. Aqua Woman, talking with seals eye to eye, that's me.

My actions caused Eva to come running back to the point and look out toward the black waters of the foggy sea with her head tilted into living question mark like a proper Australian Shepherd. When the gray seal slipped back up out of the ocean, this time just 20 feet away, I was startled, but Eva's mouth dropped wide in wonder. Her whole body wiggled. She bounced forward, giddy, into the dark water, until she was chest deep, to meet her new friend. She'd never seen a seal before.

The fog was hindering our vision. The water was ominous and black at that really deep corner where two tides collide and dig in. But Eva wasn't scared. She was certain that she'd found somebody new to play with. In that moment she trusted her gut, her intuition, the seal's body language, and maybe, my body language. She sprinted back and around the beach, looking for a stick to share, then bounded back in, hoping for a connection and holding a piece of rubbery, tube-shaped seaweed — the closest thing to a stick she could find in the moment — in her mouth as a play offering. This time the seal decided to go play with her less brave companions farther out in the water. Eva didn't take offense. She just kept walking, prancing actually, and enjoying the beach.

I was less impressed with my own seal greeting abilities after watching Eva's. I'm going to start honing my own intuition, work on trusting my gut, and on recognizing body language I can trust implicitly. Fog and darkness and difference don't necessarily mean danger. Sometimes they arrive to help you stand aware at a turning point, mouth open in wonder. Or to meet a brand new soul mate. Next time, I want to greet a new stranger smiling, curious, friendly, and chest deep in their world, not my own. Like my own personal superhero, Aqua Dog Eva, Seal Whisperer.

Jericho Brown Awakens Hearts

As a new poet, I regularly mimic great poets as a just-messing-around, poetic-calisthenics exercise. I was recently touched deeply by the work of poet Jericho Brown: specifically, his poem Heart Condition. Go find it. Read it. You won't be sorry. Better yet, be a genius and buy one of his books. In the following poem I play with everything at once, like he does, and I stick closely to the form and playfulness, even the language, of Heart Condition, because I'm a new poet, I'm learning to be as open and trusting and as honest as he is, and I just needed to hold his hand for a little while. Thank you, master poet, for awakening hearts, feelings, minds, and poets. All and at once. This is for you...

Jericho Brown Awakens Hearts

I don't want to hurt a man either, but I like to hear one vacuuming.
Two people touch twice a week, before he leaves for Seattle on the
Ferry and again when he comes back to the island. I don't dare call it
Long distance, though it feels that way. I wander the beach
Alone. Completely. Alone to ponder the fall of man, ponder privilege,
Ponder my shattered family. Content to have pain filled conversations
With myself the trees and the sea every god damn day. Every amazing
Blessed day. To solve within myself what I cannot solve out there.
Alone in our too-snug beach boots, my mother, within me, listens to
My pain. Quiet. Patient. Curious to hear what I work out for myself.
My grandmother insists on good food and doing all the work herself.
I hate to say it, but I am them. The bad, the good. I shed myself for
Mom's Alzheimer's disease. None of her. I lose none of her. I gain
More of her each day. Pull more of her up and out of me where I can
See her. I wish somebody had told me we could do that. And while
I'm at it, why could no one tell me that I'm a poet? Until my new
Island neighbors showed up this year, did just that.
God gives to each a body. A heart that breaks, falls apart. Women
Live in more than one body. We're all within each other's bodies. Wish
Somebody had told me that too. When pain mounts in my over-
Worked body, I hurt others. I research yoga classes, talk about
Writing less, exercising more.

Buy a wrist guard for the failing wrist. Keep writing. Keep talking
About doing yoga. My vocal cords are smokin' hot right now
In excellent shape from all the talking about exercise I plan to do.
One day soon my back pain will drag me kicking and screaming
To that class. Or my man will. What are you when you leave your
Man worried bout your self-inflicted pain? Who leaves their own
Wrists screaming? Jesus Christ. I do not want only the weight of our
Ancestors. I want their levity too. Their weightlessness. Want to
Float in our collective sky, creating. So I grow wings. Become the
Person who asked for help and received it. That
Fabled being who asked for forgiveness: in asking receives it. Become
Ok with going on long walks while my man vacuums.
With coming home sweaty. Alive. Ready.
Fall into housework-strengthened arms. My name is alone and strong.
I come from planet Kick Ass. I am here to learn to love myself as
Much as I love you. Here to change our name to
Team Jinda, Alzheimer's Improv Troupe #3,051,142.

Shedding Your Old Self

Here's the thing about shedding your old self. The act itself isn't hard. It's the thinking and worrying about it that's hard.

Eight years ago I thought that leaving the corporate world, the reliable paycheck, the medical benefits, and complete individual financial independence was ridiculously hard to do.

Seven years ago I worried I couldn't handle a beloved parent's diagnosis of early onset Alzheimer's disease.

Five years ago, I remember thinking that saying "No, thank you" to a job in academia (that was with amazing people — wah!) so that I could just keep writing was utterly bat-shit crazy.

Four years ago, I remember believing that giving up the idea of being a consultant to write full time was too hard.

Three years ago I worried that I simply couldn't deal with a lump in my breast at my first — very first! — mammogram.

Two years ago I remember thinking that giving up cross-neighborhood event planning would be hard (ok, this one I think was easier, I was clearly not cut out for it — it made me really bitchy). I also recall worrying that I was not cut out to parent an 8-week-old creature of any sort, ever.

Two years ago I also thought that handing over my beloved community coworking space to new people would be ridiculously tough. And I thought that letting go of my city self to become an island self would be really, really hard.

This year I worried that a parent battling depression combined with bitter squabbling in my extended family would physically break my body and my heart.

What do these things all have in common? I spent a ton of time thinking, plotting, planning, and worrying about them — almost none of which actually helped much.

Which brings me to today. Today I can't write essays.

More specifically, because technically *this* is an essay, I can't write essays for the new book I'm working on: the first book that I will be sole author on. I can only write poetry.

Day after day I sit down to write what I used to write. Day after day only poetry lands on the page. What the frack?! I am not a poet! I have no idea how to be a poet! Except for a lifetime of reading poetry, I have no training at all. Nobody is going to buy a book of poetry from a complete unknown who doesn't know what she's doing! What am I doing? And why is this fricking life not getting easier like it's supposed to if I work hard and follow my own energy?!

See.

This is what worrying alone about shedding your old self gets you: giant fearballs. These are like cat-barfed-up hairballs but made from spiraling fear and just as gross.

I've written nothing but poetry for four months straight. I'm writing poetry every day now. A poem is written even before I get out of bed, and more follow it throughout the day. I refine and edit in my dreams, wake up to make changes. This is a gift.

And worry almost caused me to miss it.

My first sole-author book will be a book of poetry.

I can't quite believe it.

Will this be hard? I have no idea, because I'm not going to worry about it or even think about it much anymore.

I'm shedding my old self again.

To the extent I can be, I will be like the baby bird escaping from its shell, the butterfly from her cocoon, and the snake from his skin. This writer is escaping from her chair to wander the world as a poet and to write wherever the breeze blows her.

The act of letting your old self go isn't the hard part.

Most days, the worrying about it is.

Life has taught me one thing, if nothing else. Worry together when you must. Don't bother worrying alone.

Sustained Creation

Writers and caregivers — and, I strongly suspect, other artists and creatives, including parents — have a different relationship with chaos and routine than other humans. We may not always love routine, but at some point in our process we recognize that we deeply need it. We may not always love chaos either, but we rapidly learn, often after some kicking and screaming and pouting about it, that we are well served by chaos, too.

I prefer the original definition of chaos (vast chasm, void) to the common modern definition (complete disarray, disorder, confusion). But whichever way you define it, chaos reminds us that we're not in control of everything, which can help us with letting go, embracing/getting past our petty sides, and lightening up. This, in turn, pulls similarly lightening-up friends to us like magnets. Together, we can then laugh and cry more often than before. Similarly lightening-up friends + more laughter + more crying together combine to allow us to find deep beauty and peace in life on good days. And they help make our worst days bearable and survivable.

What does this have to do with sustained creation? I suspect maybe everything.

It took me a while to get here, but I create constantly now. I can be found writing most days: creating essays, poems, blog posts, or books. Other days, I'm creating music, crafts, great food, home canned goods, and community play and work spaces. Sometimes alone and sometimes together. Either way, I create all the time now and with minimal worry about what I/we will create next.

I think this is possible because I've finally found, accepted, and named my individual, somewhat orderly, routine and my chaotic, collective routines. Or they found me. Either way, I honor them. I love them. I stay present for them. Even when they frustrate the holy living crap out of me. My individual routine keeps my boat afloat upon a river of sustained creation. My collective routines capsize the boat, pull me in, demand that I become the river.

Was that too woo woo? Ok, well, clarity is not my strong suit, but for the fun of it, I'll try to be explicit and clear here for a moment:

- An *individual routine* is a sequence of actions that I regularly follow. I choose to do this for myself, and it is somewhat controllable by me. I stick with it without much outside help, and sticking with it is simple when I drop my I Shoulds (which come from elsewhere, not the true me). For me, this is my daily routine as a writer and poet: 1) briefly connecting to the human world (in person or via social media), 2) disconnecting by walking with the dog and clearing my mind in nature at least twice a day, 3) drinking a beverage that makes me happy, and 4) showing up in a writing space (home office, coworking space, coffee shop) to write.

- A *collective routine* is a jumbled collection of actions that your larger self (community or family or neighborhood or organization or town or city) creates around you. A collective routine is not controllable by an individual and is chaotic by nature. Sometimes, as an individual, I feel like I don't want this one. Some days I feel like I didn't chose it, and it is way too hard. However, by recognizing it, naming it, and staying with it each day I am, in fact, choosing it, too. I choose this piece of chaos. For me, one collective routine is my routine as part of a family caregiving improv troupe centered around my parents. Team Jinda (those of us supporting them, and ourselves, in the process) is my collective center: the chaos at the heart of me. Another collective routine is my work with Daniel, my life and work partner. A third is my involvement with creating and hosting free community coworking spaces in my neighborhoods. Places where we location-independent workers gather to work, play, connect, and recharge. These are my collective routines.

Both kinds of routine deeply matter if you're interested in sustained creation. Today, most days, when I look at those massive photographic images of space that capture multiple galaxies spinning at once, I see a dancing ocean of artists' palettes, each galaxy swirling itself around a center hole into which I am certain a distant artist puts her thumb to hold on for the ride. I used to experience both chaos and the unknown as scary and something to avoid. Not so much now. Now I regularly say "Let's just do it. Try it. See what happens." So what changed?

I've shifted into experiencing everything in my life as created and needed by me: if not the individual me, then a larger me. I own my routines. And I see that one somewhat controllable, self-chosen individual routine + at least one uncontrollable collective self-chosen routine with deeply loved others as partners in crime = one very fluid and non-stop creative Lori who drips creativity in her wake as she moves most days. And in case you're wondering, yes, those deeply loved others can be annoying as hell sometimes. And you, as an individual, can be annoying as hell sometimes. These are not deal breakers for sustained creativity. Annoyances and overwhelm are helpmates. If you are overwhelmed, don't fear! You are actually in a better position to be creative than ever before! The trick is to see that.

I'm regularly asked questions such as "Don't you worry that you'll run out of things to write about?" and "How do you keep coming up with new things to say?" If you are asking questions like these, it's possible that you have moved into over-focusing on yourself as an individual, on having complete control, and it might be time to consider switching things up by finding, naming, and honoring your collective, chaotic routines. Give more energy and time to your collective self — your community or your family or your city, for example — reconnect with the routines that remind you you're not in control, tip you upside down, and shake you up a bit.

On the other end of the spectrum, I also often get asked questions like "How do you stay so focused?" or "How do you find the time to write?" or "Out of everything you could possibly write about, how do you decide what to do next?" If you are asking questions like these, it's possible that you have moved into over-focusing on your collective self and are neglecting your individual self (a far-too-easy thing to do for caregivers, yes?). It took me 40 years to realize that I — as an individual — am allowed to be in the top 10 on my priorities list. If this sounds familiar, in this moment you will serve everyone better — everyone — by reprioritizing your individual self a bit. Doesn't have to be a big thing at first. When I slip on this one, I remember that my writing and I are important by making myself a special, fancy tea, writing with a favorite pen in a favorite notebook instead of on my laptop, and giving myself 5 minutes of free Lori time to just hang out with that hot beverage and lovely pen. Or, if I have just 2 minutes, I play by writing #micropoetry on Twitter. Because writing is the best Lori recharge engine there is and to utterly abandon it is a mistake. There are many more Lori rechargers, but I'm talking about prioritizing yourself and what you love even on the busiest, hardest, and worst days of your life. On those days, 2 minutes of me-time is needed so I don't entirely lose touch with my grateful-for-life self.

I've watched my life long enough now that I can see that honoring my individual and collective routines usually allows me to find beauty in chaos. Even on the day last month that Daniel lost his job and mom was in the hospital again and we had to face telling our friends living in our Seattle home that we had to sell the home. The same day there was yet another school shooting in my gun-worshiping/children's-rights ignoring country. The same day that the dog jumped up onto the bed, onto me, before she barfed. There was deep beauty in that day moving alongside the pain and gagging as I cleaned barf off my pajamas. And I could feel it.

Routine is often misunderstood. Self-chosen routine isn't for the timid. And it isn't about taming or controlling chaos either. It isn't ultimately about constraint at all. Self-chosen routine is about giving myself more space and time, and coming to understand myself enough, that I know how to open my eyes to all of what is, not just part of it. About knowing how to move myself into a state of being that is me again: conscious, aware, and able to recognize beauty in almost everything. The beauty of chaos when I'm in the state to see it is tough to capture with words alone. The closest word I can think of is "Wheee!" combined with that excited, empty-pit-of-stomach feeling we get when leaping from a great height while fairly certain that we'll land safely. Words fail.

So back to sustained creation…

It's because of my connection to unending beauty, and to the pain of living, that I don't fear running out of things to write, ideas to try, things to say, ways to be, people to know, friends to make, options to see, perspectives to consider, work to do, and so on. Within unfathomable chaos is unending abundance. And I regularly stand in chaos and look around. When connected to unending abundance, I also don't fear looking stupid, because I know the very next moment I could look like a total genius (neither of which most people will ever notice anyway). Looking stupid is no big thing when anything is possible the very next moment.

Self-chosen routine also gives me the limits I need to find focus, recognize when it's time to re-create something, create something new, and decide when something is finished for now.

I can hear the loving voices of my mountain of social justice-centered friends in my head. They tell me that not everybody has access to self-chosen routine. That to have it is a privilege. I hear you and I believe you, friends. And my perspective is that everybody has access to self-chosen routine because for me access to the infinite comes from within us. I watch as Viktor Frankl walks out of a Nazi concentration camp with a self-chosen deep faith in humanity. His parents, his wife, his brother all tortured to death at the hands of their captors. Even with all apparent power in the world, they couldn't take away what he chose for himself. So bad ass!

I find great power in deciding to see both my individual routine and my chaotic collective routines as chosen by me (individual me and larger me). No matter what the world is doing around me. Because I see them all as chosen by me, I'm the one who gets to make changes at will. I'm not stuck waiting on somebody else to change. I imagine these routines as temporary structures that allow chaos to show up for me today in personally receivable chunks. They help increase the chances that I'll notice beauty. And increase the likelihood of me raising my voice and calling "Bullshit" when I don't. I can think of self-chosen routines as the tap on the faucet and one place that I can reliably go for water. Not that I experience self-chosen routine as easy for humans. It takes a lot of selves, pulling together, to make self-chosen routine possible here in Lori Land. They also mean more vulnerability and more asking for help than I tend to be comfortable with as an individual.

Without self-chosen routine, I get stuck in the mud of chaos. Chaos can then make me feel like a tiny, helpless, trapped creature. To the point that the idea of connecting to unending beauty sounds like a pipe dream, a fantasy, or a ridiculous and cruel joke. And the idea of being a good poet, writer, caregiver, wife, sister, daughter, or neighbor in this messed-up world can feel like both an up-hill battle and a completely lost cause.

In our family, there has been discussion this year about what makes somebody an artist. The artist men in my life have practically come to blows on the subject, which has made me laugh out loud on more than one occasion. I imagine our cats thinking "Artist fight!" Men. God love'm. As if it was important to agree.

For me, being an artist has to do with what we value. Fishermen value fish, fishing, feeding others, and the culture of fishing. Farmers value the earth, the weather, farming, food, feeding others, and the farming culture. Their routines reflect what they value. Artists value creation, including human creation, in its many guises, and feeding the human spirit, and we're drawn to people who like to talk about humans and animals as creators and makers and crafters. Those recognized by others as artists dedicate themselves to their creations, and their individual routine, at least, reflects that. But to recognize ourselves as artists is something else entirely. It requires dedication to our chaotic collective routines. To our larger selves. Our individual routine revolves around creation to the extent it can–an act that pushes open our tiny door to infinity and then closes it. The choice to prioritize your own collective chaotic routines keeps the door open.

To have sustained creation in my life, I needed sustained access to the infinite.

Tapping into the infinite may feel like magic some days, but sustained creation isn't a trick. And it doesn't feel like a talent or a strength or a privilege most days, either. Sustained creation is about valuing creation, and your part in it, so much that you prioritize creation and co-creation regularly, despite the odds and with all your individual fears and problems and responsibilities along for the ride. Sustained creation is about prioritizing what you love to create (even as that shifts) and who you love (even as that shifts) and allowing and inviting others around you to do the same.

The act of recognizing, naming, and owning both my individual routine and my crazy-ass collective routines has allowed creation itself to become my routine, while being supported by, and supporting others, doing the same. It's been about learning to let go and move on to the next thing when a voice from my own doorway says "Enough. Done. At least for now." And about learning to never give up on the humans and the work I love most — even when they're impossible. Even when they're me.

Simple, right?

5. The Joy and Power of Groundless Beings

Welcome to the Void

so welcome here
sitting in the sun at a rusty table
lunch with caregivers
in front of Useless Bay
sparrows bathe in dust at our feet
fluff and primp without shame
we admire their audacity

together we swing across Alzheimer's
through marriage troubles
creative projects
travel
waistlines
back into Alzheimer's seamlessly
belly laughs to tears
nuts and bolts to wild imaginings
pain, fear, and giggling back out of ourselves

someone says "I can see when she is leaving
this space-time continuum."

I think "Yes! That's it!"

our beautiful, beautiful multiselves
grateful we don't have to watch this process from a distance
on the Sci-Fi channel
captive to the imagination of strangers

we live this. we who were
born to be space travelers
born to be many
born to weep together publicly
born to swing across space, beyond memory, outside time,
across selves

content with patchwork ships of friends and duct tape
we have all the time in the world here
I notice now
just home from a 4-hour lunch outside space time self
yet still entirely home

the void, chaos, the space between us: emptiness herself is home now

I am welcome here.
No, that's not quite it, space travelers.

here, I *am* welcome

so welcome, friends

welcome to the void

Second Wife

Dear spouse,

I want to tell you about grief. No, I don't.
I want to tell you about me – the woman emerging from the ocean
in winter, naked.
The wife you loved and knew died in my arms yesterday.
You'll be living with me now: Wife 2.0. Lucky man.

First the good news.

I couldn't care less where you leave your socks and shoes.
Don't care when or if you ever do your dishes.
I think weeds are lost, misunderstood yard angels.
That sand on the floor should be sculpted
into intricate art installations
at least as often as it is mindlessly swept away.
I enjoy wearing the same cozy sweater for days on end while I create
I don't like doing laundry. Stains are more misunderstood angels
ideal brooch locations.

Hmm. Maybe that was the bad news. Let me try again.
First the good news.

When you can't find me
I may be on the beach looking at rocks
on my hands and knees
tumbling words in my poet's mind like the most devoted lapidarist.
Words are cool. Stones hold words for those who look.

Most days you'll find me at my writing desk.
Epic tales. In pajamas. Poems everywhere.

When life really sucks
you might find me reading strange books, watching strange TV
last month I watched all 153 episodes of Gilmore Girls on Netflix,
in rapid succession, to mend my heart when my extended family
shattered.

I feel no shame. No guilt.
All my experience is gift. All of it.
Rory and Lorelai Gilmore were there
when grief burned my branches bare.
Silly, imperfect help is plenty.
You won't catch this wife judging your taste in entertainment.
Our hearts know who and what they need to heal. I'll trust yours to
look after you.

I offer one tip.

Don't worry about me. Just don't.
Some days I may appear lost and alone.
That's part of me. A part I love.

I am an explorer. I take my time.
I move through The Museum of Modern Loss with wonder
Whoa. What? Huh. Wow.
Pain and grief are T-Rex bones in the rotunda.
Vulnerabilities are just strengths that I widened to
reveal, revel in, more of me.
When my skin gets too small I move toward them
crack myself open to step through new. Whole.
Doesn't make me a chicken. Or a dinosaur.
When I need rest, I take it (see *Gilmore Girls*, above).
Or I get a wrist guard. Or I ask for help.
This wife asks for help when she needs it. Please let me ask.

Ok, so that was two tips. Now the bad news.

You're married to an artist now.
Living a textbook case for use of the expression "Man up."
Artists pull forth new worlds. Find comfort in chaos.
Stand still at the heart of hell to burn, listen, record for remembrance,
chase fireflies.
Our hands our heads our hearts all equals
This makes us absentminded some days. Messy most.
My train even more choo choo — tough to — follow that thought.

Fully engage your heart to hear me now. And your funny bone.
And your home-keeping skills. And your improvisation skills.

An artist will not try to engage parts of you for you. That's on you.
I am engaged with myself.

Shit. Maybe that was the good news. I don't know. You tell me...

Grieve her in your way, as you must.
You knew her well, that woman: the one inclined
to weep over messes and rage about dirty dishes.
I can't.

The gifts of rage and weeping will not be wasted on dust and cutlery
in this house.

Screw it, honey, the dishes will keep.

Today we dance.

The Joy of "I Don't Know"

While cleaning my office this morning I found an old journal called *Gratitude: A Journal*. It actually says that on its salmon-colored cover and spine. According to the first entry, I got it in July 2009 — and when I touched it I recalled that at the time I bought one for me, one for my mom, and one for my sister — at a time when we were all deeply freaked out about Mom's Alzheimer's diagnosis.

I'm only about 20 pages into its 200-ish blank pages. Not that that means I've only been grateful 20 times in the past 7 years. Its lack of use has to do with the journal's thickness and postcard size. It's uncomfortable to write in — especially for someone like me who likes to wend along, exploring the mystery, taking my time as I write.

Or maybe that's not a problem. Because I now notice what this journal is actually good for. When I occasionally find it again, it's a great place for creating a Top 10 Things I'm Grateful for Right Now list.

Today, in the fall of 2015, my Top 10 grateful-for list is this:

1. The still ocean out my window

2. The sounds of Daniel downstairs, cooking something in the kitchen

3. Batman the cat on my lap

4. The amazing generosity of our friends/renters, who tried to get me to stay for dinner, and spend the night last night, by bribing me with home-cooked Thai food at our/their Seattle house

5. That Mom is out of the hospital today, comfortable at home again

6. That Dad is allowing Daniel and I to drive their car here to the island this week. Allowing us to help! And moving here! Double hooray!

7. The peppermint tea in my mug

8. Cool air and rain after a spookily dry and hot summer

9. The three artist friends — and dozen non-artist friends — who leapt in with offers to help me with the book cover this week, when our original artist needed to step away to take care of herself

10. Our savvy and kind real estate agent and all the other humans on earth who thrive serving others in ways I'm not good at and doing things I totally suck at. Go humanity!

11. Oooo! Egg potato onion bacon frittata! Thanks honey.

In September 2013, this was my gratitude Top 10 list:

1. Stories and articles shared by women friends

2. Friends who want to be interviewed for our new book

3. Eva the dog

4. The cats

5. Writing + my laptop + iPad

6. Green tea, especially matcha

7. Hearing about the lives of friends and family

8. Planet Earth

9. Daniel and Bas

10. Play

As I look back at my old lists across 7 years, it's fascinating how a Top 10 grateful list changes with time. What stays important. What shifts.

In mine, friends are always mentioned, as are pets, writing, Daniel, and some form of beverage (I've been thankful for coffee, juice, and Chai tea lattes other years).

My parents and sister are mentioned almost every time as well. Bas, you were mentioned in 2011, 2012, and 2013. I think that makes you family. Go team orange!

Housemates, coworkers, and other friends, new and old, are mentioned periodically as well. I tend to be thankful for those I'm living and working with that moment.

I also tend to be thankful for the weather — interestingly to me, whatever weather it happens to be at the moment I'm writing. Sunshine, fog, or rain, I'm grateful for it when I'm writing.

So the things that persist over time and appear again and again in these lists must be what I'm most grateful for. What matters most to me. Hmmm.

****

The following is the end of this piece exactly as it existed when I first wrote it back in 2013. A small part of me wishes I could go back in time and tell 2013 Lori that she will come out ok. That she will soon be happier and stronger than she's ever felt (although I'd leave out the part about hot flashes showing up at 45). I'd tell her that her desire to walk beside the ocean will lead her family to move to an amazing island where they gratefully walk beside the ocean every day surrounded by new friends and neighbors they love. Then again, there's a certain freedom, awakening power, and joy within her I Don't Know. Within the I Don't Know, there's a sliver of We've Got This. And the tiniest thread, I've since learned, is more than enough...

****

I'm moving into a new phase of my life right now: a massive paring down phase. A phase in which I'm more deeply aware of what matters to me and prioritizing what matters most — giving what matters most a lot more space and letting other things go.

This summer I've let go of all work commitments that I don't have energy for anymore. And after a flurry of traveling in early summer, since then I've been very still. I don't want to go anywhere. I don't want to do anything. Well, not nothing. I want to sit. I want to write. I want to listen to the silence and the wind blowing through the trees.

Play with the pets. Watch Sci-Fi. Make matcha smoothies. Walk beside the ocean.

Our society has many negative words associated with this period I've been in that I could accept if I chose to: Procrastination. Laziness. Sloth. Depression.

But that's not what this is.

This is Stillness. Reflection. Fallow time. Part of Wayfinding.

This is what I needed after I lost myself this spring and no amount of busy-ness, flailing, or complaining my way out worked.

What I really needed to do was notice.

Notice what matters to me now.

Notice where I fit now. Notice who and what I am.

Now.

And then to become ok, again, simply with what is.

To notice and become ok again, I need stillness, reflection, fallow time. The bigger the change, the more I need.

Back in April I was full of guilt and apology for needing this space and time. But August me, the new me, took the time, without guilt and with very little apology. Without thinking there is something wrong with me for changing or for needing what I need. My fallow time was time well spent.

I now know that I always have time for writing and story gathering. Always time for Daniel, Eva, and the cats. Always time for play. Always time for tea or coffee.

I noticed that many things that used to bring me a great deal of joy just don't anymore. Some were easy to let go of: like work that was clearly not for me anymore. And some things — in particular, taking care of our large home and yard and garden — are much harder to let go of. This work has been a huge part of me the past 12 years.

This was work I happily took on in 2002 when I bought this house, gleefully took on even more of when I leapt away from the corporate world in 2007, and joyfully took on even more of when I turned our home into a Coworking space in February 2012.

What does it mean for us that taking care of our home, yard, and garden don't bring today-me the joy that they used to? Is it time to sell the house? Find a caretaker? Allow Mother Nature to take back her yard? Close the Coworking space? Is it time to hit the road — packing Daniel, Eva, Bella, Batman, and Joe up to go with me?

I just don't know.

I don't know.

And what's really interesting about right now is that I notice that this new me doesn't want to solve this not knowing.

I don't want to experience this not knowing as a problem, so I'm not.

I'm ok with not knowing. I'm ok. Most days.

I know what matters most to me now. I have it within my power to give what does matter all the time and space it needs. So why would I want to get rid of this precious "I don't know" too quickly? I am a person with five intentionally empty shelves in her 6-shelf office bookcase, because I love the openness and mystery of blank space, potential, and possibility even more than I love books.

My I Don't Know allows me to become an empty shelf, become the possibility, become the mystery that I love.

I Don't Know means that I am aware, reflecting, changing, and opening to what will show up next.

I may not know where I'm going or exactly what I'm doing next — I may never know — but I know who and what I'm taking with me.

For today me, that's more than enough.

Our Disease, Our Story

Ten years have passed since we first noticed significant changes in Mom. Eight years since the official doctor's diagnosis: Alzheimer's disease. Back then we blindly accepted the experts' truths, stories, and definitions as our own. We picked up the following traditional definition, for example, as if God herself had etched it into a large boulder and dropped it unforgivingly on our heads…

According to the Alzheimer's Foundation (March 2015), Alzheimer's disease is *a progressive, degenerative disorder that attacks the brain's nerve cells, or neurons, resulting in loss of memory, thinking and language skills, and behavioral changes.* According to Bright Focus (March 2015), in people who have been diagnosed, its progress is commonly tracked in three stages:

- **Mild (Stage 1).** People with Alzheimer's tend to first exhibit minor memory loss and mood swings and are slow to learn and react. They start to shy away from anything new and prefer the familiar. Patients can still perform basic tasks but may need assistance with more complicated activities. Speech and understanding become slower, and patients often lose their train of thought. They may get lost while traveling or forget to pay bills. As they become aware of this loss of control, they may become depressed, fearful, irritable, and restless.

- **Moderate (Stage 2).** Eventually, people with the illness begin to be disabled by it. Though the distant past may be recalled, recent events become difficult to remember. Advancing Alzheimer's affects the ability to comprehend location, the day, and the time. Caregivers must give clear instructions and repeat them often. As Alzheimer's patients' minds continue to slip away, they may invent words and not recognize formerly familiar faces.

- **Severe (Stage 3).** During the final stage, patients become less and less responsive. Memory becomes so poor that no one is recognizable. Patients lose bowel and bladder control and eventually need constant care. They lose the ability to chew and swallow, and become vulnerable to pneumonia, infection, and other illnesses. Respiratory problems worsen, particularly when the patient becomes bedridden. This stage eventually leads to coma and death.

Wow. No wonder we were terrified at the beginning. Some major changes were happening in a beloved family member, we went to our culture's healers for help, and this was the story we were handed: a half story. A victim's story.

In this half story, Mom instantly became something less: a slipping-away *patient* doomed to decline, frustration, pain, coma, and death. And all the rest of us became something less too: caregivers. People in non-stop give mode – no longer part of life's dance of giving and receiving. In the case of Alzheimer's disease, being a caregiver means something worse. It's akin to being a long-term helpless bystander: someone who gets to spend years (if you're lucky) busily dusting bookshelves on The Titanic.

Without the wholeness of context, experience, and community – without the whole story – the natural response to having this horror of a half story thrust upon you by a healer is some combination of fear, dread, anger, denial, anxiety, and depression. It's no wonder that people resist going to doctors to get this diagnosis. It's no wonder that doctors hesitate to share this diagnosis once they make it. Offering a half story to already terrified people isn't healing.

Here in our family, we're 10+ years in now. We're not living somebody else's story anymore. We're living our own story. And while I happily support other healers in our culture by doing Alzheimer's fundraising walks, signing up for research trials, and donating money for research and support, what I won't do anymore is sit quietly by as if the half story is enough.

We're all so much more. We deserve better.

At 45, I still feel like a kid much of the time, yet I'm a family elder now. I'm a family healer now, too, within my own family. If I still used the traditional definitions, I'd tell you that my mom entered the Moderate (Stage 2) phase of the disease about 2 years ago. But I rarely use half stories anymore.

Being a family elder and healer involves deep listening and deep gratitude. Listening to Mom, Dad, my sister and her husband, myself and my husband as individuals and as a whole. Watching what we do. How we do things. What we eat. Where we go. How we feel. How we change. How we help each other. Reflecting deeply on what is happening with us. I also watch and listen to our neighbors, closest family members, and friends. And to other families with similar diagnoses. I watch what we all do. How we all do things. I notice our impact on each other. I reflect on what is happening with those around us as a whole too. I feel deep gratitude for all these people – even those my immediate family has had to say goodbye-for-now to – because we're all part of the whole.

Instead of fighting a planet of doctors on this, which I don't have time for, I think it's simpler to say that today, from my perspective, my mom's initial diagnosis was wrong. Or, no, I'll be more generous and say that it was half right.

Mom doesn't have just Alzheimer's disease.

Mom also has Linda's disease.

Linda's disease is *a progressive, generative, advanced state of familying in which the closest family members and friends begin spending a lot more time together as adults, staying in the present moment more often together, laughing more, sharing and letting go of fears together, experimenting with new ideas and activities and selves, shedding unnecessary stuff and pain-generating people and places without guilt, communicating far more than before and learning to intuitively, almost telepathically, communicate with and support one another and a growing circle of emotionally close others. By mid-stage, Linda's disease cracks open core family members' imaginations and transforms them into powerful new selves — for example, into artists, advocates, activists, poets, parents, grandparents, dancers, care partners, play-event inventors, game creators, and group improvisation experts. The bravest family member slowly becomes a living, word-free guru (or guide, or angel, if you prefer): helping the others shed their burdens and live more awake, aware, brave, and beautiful lives. Eventually, everyone in the core family and closely connected to them receives similar living-guru/guide/angel gifts and shares them with others — across cultures and other imagined boundaries — yet closely connected to themselves.*

Linda's disease holds the potential to transform our entire planet for the better. Or at the very least, to transform us for the better.

This is the other half of the story for us.

Yes, Alzheimer's disease is harder than hell — especially within an immature culture and medical system that often appears to value money above living beings and people for the things they produce instead of simply for who they are and their amazing existence and experience right now.

Our more whole story is the one that truly honors Mom for who she is today: a woman who reminds us of the deep healing potential of putting on a fluffy robe, doing dishes together, drawing pictures together, and laughing together. A woman who doesn't need fancy clothes, fancy titles, important work, or even a well-functioning brain to experience the world as utterly, jaw-droppingly amazing most days. All she needs is love, and she draws it to herself, and to us, brilliantly and simply, teaching us more and more about ourselves all the time. More than 10 years into her disease.

Healers, I don't have to tell you that sharing only half a story with people already terrified and struggling can do harm.

Families and friends, I don't have to tell you that living only half a story, a victim's story — somebody else's story handed to you from a distance — can do harm too.

Today we're being called to live and create our own stories: stories in which we're characters in the tale and also authors, creators, of the tale. Tales in which we all get a voice, including those who communicate without words. Tales that don't stop half way through, stranding us as victims. Tales in which family members and elders and healers and neighbors and others going on similar journeys play and work hand-in-hand as equals.

We are all so much more than the old story told us we were.

How do I know this?

Because we're 10+ years into our own transformation. Over the years since the diagnosis, Mom has given us more of herself, not less, than in the past. Without saying a word, she's given me the courage to leave energy-draining corporate work, to turn our home into a community coworking space, to become an author, to move to an island when I felt called to do so but didn't know why, and to recognize myself as a poet. She helped return me to myself: the girl painting rocks and sitting on the beach writing poetry. She helped return my sister to herself too: giving her the courage to become a mother herself this year, despite her fears. We can hear Mom's voice within us now, and feel her story and ours weaving together, whether we're in the same room or thousands of miles apart.

Our story. *Our* words. *Our* definitions.

Here at Moderate (Stage 2) of Linda's Disease, we may invent words and stories and selves and definitions for ourselves, not only because we have to but because we can. We may no longer recognize familiar faces because we have shed our former selves and become something both oddly familiar and yet entirely new together. Here we may begin to tell the other half of the Alzheimer's disease story: the half that "well" people in our culture cannot imagine or see without us. Because here, right here, we live and play and dance and laugh and weep together. Here we are whole. Here we become our potential.

Right here. In the middle of the glorious mess that is us.

This is the moment we become game changers.

Five Crappy Ideas that Alzheimer's Shattered

I spent last week with Mom and Dad for Mom's St. Patrick's Day birthday week. We had a fantastic time! We went dancing and their neighbors taught me the two-step and how to line dance. We went to Assisted Living: The Musical, to a friend's choral concert, and rocked out one night at the Arizona Opry. We drove up into the mountains for lunch — stopping along the way to look at wildflowers and views. We also hung out with neighbors during several happy hours, made cookies and bars and margaritas for a party, and shopped for necessities. They wore me out.

We've been living with Mom's Alzheimer's diagnosis for a decade now. For years after the diagnosis, I was terrified. Mostly — it now seems — because I believed my culture's shallow, distant hype back then about a lot of things. For example, back then I blindly, unquestioningly, believed that:

1. Slowing down means falling behind

2. Losing our independence means losing our value or worth

3. Dropping our filters and inhibitions means embarrassment and loss of dignity

4. Letting go of speech means losing our ability to communicate

5. Losing our minds means losing our selves

Wow. What a gigantic load of bullshit I allowed my culture to dump, unexamined, into my head. Fortunately, our family functions like a sea sponge most days now: that kind of crap flows in, through us, and right on out the other side...

1. Slowing down means falling behind – this idea is hooey

Slowing down with our parents and each other has meant we've all had to let go of a lot of ideas and former selves and old responsibilities. Mom and Dad let go of being the always-there-helping-us-all-the-time-in-person family elders they once were. They prioritized themselves for a change: they had to. They moved to a warmer climate. Started playing bingo every Tuesday and dancing every Friday. They started having happy hours with neighbors every other day or so. Started laughing out loud often, and every day, like they did back when they were first married. Recently they started getting and enjoying reading the newspaper every day again. Dad reads the Funnies out loud to Mom. It's beautiful to watch. Between that and the Internet, he's more up-to-date on current affairs in this country than just about anyone I know — including my always-up-to-date activist friends across Seattle.

Slowing down has unleashed a series of tremendous gifts for Daniel and me too. There is no judgment here about your life choices: everybody's life and slowing down looks different. This is just what our slowing down looks like...

A year after Mom's diagnosis, I quit my full-time job to finish a degree instead of trying to do both at once like I'd done in the past. Soon after that, I gave up my pursuit of traditional business consulting and instead turned our home into a free community coworking space — embracing a true-for-me idea that community and closer relationships with neighbors were what we/I really needed. Slowing down even further with neighbors regularly in our home, I re-learned about the gift economy and swapping, sharing, re-imagining, and bartering: things I'd completely forgotten as options. Eventually I began writing books, because I finally had time to notice that I'm a writer.

We later moved outside the city and slowed down even more. Here I became a poet and Daniel began hosting photography workshops out of our home. This year, we created our first flash nonfiction book, in just 4 weeks, using found-object art and already gathered community stories. We can move like lightening now when the community needs us to. We now have the space/time/ability to respond in a flash to community needs and also the ability to say "No, we can't be involved with this right now." without guilt. All because we slowed down.

2. Losing our independence means losing our value or worth – also hooey

Losing our independence has meant Mom and Dad growing closer as time goes on. It's meant a shift to a 55+ community where they have more dear friends — friends available to them round the clock — and within-walking-distance activities and services. Meant sharing cooking and housework responsibilities and bringing in extra help as needed. Meant a traditional dad — inclined to listen to his own voice as decider and leader — learning to listen more closely and becoming more able to intuitively understand what Mom needs. He even began listening to his daughters more, too, who have a lot more to offer than he realized before. Our parents matter more to each other, and more to us, and we matter more to them, thanks to Alzheimer's disease.

Losing our independence has meant my sister and I growing closer as the years pass, instead of farther apart, even though we live three states away from each other and have different interests, goals, and work lives. It's meant growing closer to our own husbands, and to each other's husbands, and to our core-circle friends too. It's meant becoming even more honest with and growing closer to neighbors. And making friends with other care partners: people we can share literally anything with. Losing our independence has meant a continuous revealing of our interdependence. A continuous revealing of our individual fears, our hidden beliefs and ideas, and our inner selves. Everyone still in our lives today matters more to us now, not less. And for those who've stuck with us through our worst, we matter more to them now, too.

3. Dropping our filters and inhibitions means embarrassment and loss of dignity – so much hooey

Mom doesn't remember names anymore. Yet when she spots people she knows she may sprint across the store, or the parking lot, or the yard to greet them. She often embraces people she knows with full-body joy. On occasion, she may even hug somebody she doesn't know. Each moment I set aside my own uptight concerns about this, something new comes into focus: most people adore being greeted this way. Mom can pull smiles and laughter out of anyone now, including strangers. Many of her neighbors light up when they see her coming, saying "Yay! Here comes my hug!" The rest of us don't give each other enough credit. She does. She greets people the way I've always wished I could: with the full joy and abandon and pureness of spirit of a puppy. Her dignity isn't lost. If anything, she points out how far the rest of us have to go.

Mom adores singing and can remember a lot more when she does. She sings along during concerts and musicals now — even when nobody else in the audience is singing. Early on, this embarrassed me. Now I join her. I began noticing that often other people start to sing when she does. We choose concerts and musical events now where we're surrounded by people who see the genius in singing along to life instead of being an audience of silent observers. Places where audience participation isn't welcome aren't places we want to be anyway.

Last week while we were sitting in their retirement community's Jacuzzi one evening, with 7 or 8 other people we didn't know, Mom closed her eyes, cupped her hands, and began slowly lifting and pouring water over her head repeatedly — in pure, un-bothered-by-others bliss at the feel of the warm water on a cool night — as if she was alone in her own bathtub. At first I felt a little embarrassed. I asked her if she was cold and wanted a towel. But she wasn't cold. She was just doing her own thing and enjoying the moment differently. I made a conscious effort to get over myself and then I just watched. She was beautiful.

Embarrassment is my burden to let go of, not hers. She's light-years ahead of me. Mom carries with her the wisdom of the Buddha, the Christ, the Woman, and the Child now.

In her presence, I learn to let go of my burdens.

4. Letting go of speech means losing the ability to communicate – total crap this one

Much of Mom's spoken language is gone now. She listens most of the time instead of speaking. Answering most questions as an individual is beyond her. When she does speak, it's usually in short, 1- to 4-word phrases about what's happening in the present moment. A traditional way to look at this (in my culture) is to believe that Mom needs help with conversation. Dad, Jen, I, and others close to her serve as conversation supporters: interpreting and filling in the blanks in what she's trying to say. When strangers or neighbors ask questions, she starts by saying a few words, we fill in a sentence or two, she continues adding a few more, and so on. It's actually really fun most days to communicate together like this. It feels like a game.

Another way to look at this is to see Mom as a teacher of listening, collective communication, and even telepathy. She's training us to be more intuitive, better listeners, better interpreters, more patient, more creative and imaginative, and to experience all communication as a service to a greater whole. She's also teaching us to sing more often.

I hear Mom in my head more than I ever have before. I can be walking on the beach — four states away from her — and still hear her. Whether I'm creating poetry, a grocery list, or working out a problem in my head, she's with me now. Her voice and her stories live in my head alongside the voice I identify as my own and the voices of my grandmothers. Many people only open to an experience like this after the death of a loved one. Thanks to Alzheimer's disease, I get to experience many years of this while Mom's still around in person.

I don't mean to downplay the frustrations of losing the ability to speak. It can be really frustrating. And at the moment I find great joy in noticing that Mom can go days and weeks at a time now — here at mid stage — without appearing to be frustrated about this at all. She's relaxed into the idea of collective communication and listening. She's satisfied with hugs and smiles and singing and group improvisation. And so am I. I find that 99% of our time together now is about the pure joy of being together.

5. Losing our minds means losing our selves – the biggest hooey of them all

Mom has taught me that wherever the "self" lives, it's not as rigidly tied to the individual mind and the brain as I was once certain it was. At her core, wherever that is, Mom is a smiling, kind, happy, helpful, funny, singing, honest, occasionally crying, occasionally jealous, yet always generous soul. The most terrifying part about Alzheimer's disease was the idea that we would be losing the woman we know, love, and recognize entirely — that a disease of the brain would literally erase her from existence bit by bit as we watched, helpless.

It's not as simple as that. Alzheimer's isn't easy. Yes, and…

Alzheimer's has wiped away some parts of Mom while revealing and giving to us the core of her. Mom was once whip smart and had a great memory, but we didn't love her for her intellect and her recall. She was an expert planner and record keeper and home keeper and cook, but we didn't love her for those things either. Our love grew out of a shared recognition that we were free to be our true selves together. Our selves were free to join her smiling, kind, happy, helpful, funny, singing, honest, occasionally crying or jealous, yet always generous self. This is still true. In fact, most days, it feels a lot simpler now than it did 10 years ago. Because the disease hasn't just knocked away some parts of Mom: it's been knocking away parts of me and Jen and Dad that didn't serve us well either. We can move from our core selves now and as a collective self now. The days we do are really good days.

I was just in Arizona for Mom's St. Patrick's Day birthday week. We were standing at a large department-store counter while a woman blew up a bouquet of green balloons for us for a party their neighbors were throwing. I noticed a big Disney princess display full of gifts for girls. I pointed at the display and said "Mom, how'd you like a princess fleece blanket for your birthday?" She smiled, put her arm around me, and said "I don't need that. You girls are my princesses." We hugged each other tight then: both perfectly content and oblivious to the clamor of the too-busy department store. We were both completely aware of what a deep gift the other's presence is. Mom spoke back-to-back complete sentences to me in that moment: the only time she did so during my 5-day visit.

I will never forget that gift, that moment. How we pulled ourselves outside of time together.

Thanks to Mom's disease, we've become more fully present in the moment together. We notice the tiniest of amazing things now. We're grateful for the tiniest of things now. Mom is still right here with me, beside me, within me, arm around me. Still fluidly helping me and teaching me, laughingly or silently, often invisibly. We are unbelievably lucky to be living this life, to have each other, and we know it.

We haven't lost ourselves at all. We've found ourselves together.

How Do I Get Family Members to Offer Better/Different Support?

We've been living with Mom's Alzheimer's disease for 9 years now. I can't believe she's still with us. Still knows us. Laughs with us. Helps where she can (teaching, for example, of the extraordinary joy to be found in folding warm, just-out-of-the-dryer laundry). We are so lucky. These days I occasionally receive questions from other care partners and family members living with this disease too. I decided to blog my answers online, as questions come up, to save us time. Here's the first one: actually four that are variations on a theme.

Question:

How do I make my other family members:

- help my family member with Alzheimer's disease?
- help me?
- do their fair share?
- offer better/very different support than they're offering now?

My response:

Dementia care partner, I'm sorry, but you don't. You don't have the time and energy to bother with trying to make other people do things. Welcome aboard the S.S. That Ship Has Sailed. I used to think I could make other people do things. That me spent hours, days, and, in some cases, years, trying and failing miserably at this. That's not me anymore. Thank you, Alzheimer's.

Try this instead. It actually works. Plus, it creates precious time instead of taking it.

1. **drop old expectations**. Ideally, actually physically drop them. Write them down on paper, crinkle that paper into a ball, and drop it on the ground. Step on it for good measure. Or toss it in the fireplace and watch it burn.

2. **begin to notice and surround yourself with people, experiences, and things that are more naturally really good at helping you**. For example, the friends who've been care partners before, other care partners online, social organizations that get it, neighbors who get it, books, blogs, dogs, cats, children, playful adults, trees, birds, sunbeams, local support groups, professional help, fresh air, and chocolate. Look at all the people/creatures/beings/things who can actually help!

3. **let go, for now, of the people who drain your much needed and very precious care partner energy**. This includes the old you. Say a fond farewell to them and to the you who thought she could make other people do things, failed, got disappointed, got angry, and then got tired. It was so strange. That day. The day I realized that Mom's disease wasn't making me tired. My own expectations, anger, and disappointment — in myself and other family members — was. Most days.

4. **use the time you receive wisely**. Your heart knows what you need. What feels good? Rage? Rest? Reflection? Use your new worry-free moments to re-find you. This becomes possible again when you utterly surround yourself with you-centered energy creators. This might mean new people, fewer people, new experiences, fewer experiences, new things, and/or fewer things around you. Let your heart be your doorman. Your bouncer. People allowed in your door now are those who you create energy with. You literally feel your heart lighten up when you see them. Get over what you SHOULD be doing. The people and creatures who actually light up your heart are your people now. Find them. Stick with them. Or be your most-honest, true, vulnerable self as visibly as you can, and they'll find you.

Our story:

In the early stage, for years, we tried keeping the whole extended family together, across thousands of miles in some cases. We'd been a close-knit loving family of 40ish gentle, sweet, and ridiculously conflict-adverse mid-westerners. By mid stage, however, the care requirements for both Mom and for failing-health-primary-caregiver

Dad, grew time-consuming enough that we failed at extended family communication. We didn't just fail. We failed spectacularly. We had to become ok with a rift across the extended family. Dad snapped, turned on some family members and they turned on him, and some relationships shattered.

Here at mid stage, for us to thrive, it takes three groups of people:

1. **The A team.** The 10ish-member tight care partner improvisation troupe, willing to laugh together, work together and love each other no matter what. We call ourselves Team Jinda. Professional house-cleaning and other assistance has joined the team too.

2. **The B team.** The 20+-member love-from-a-distance team, the family who still loves us and checks in with us via Skype, Facebook, and by sending words of encouragement now and then. They boost our spirits from time to time in person and also when we think about them. They are providing support to both the A team and the C team now, so they, too, have their hands full.

3. **The C team.** The 10ish-member has-to-move-away-for-now team. These friends and relatives have enough heartache and worries of their own that they can't handle us as we are right now and/or we can't handle them. They have their hands full too. We love them and don't blame them. And the A team had to break contact with them to focus on caregiving and keeping care partners strong. Fortunately for us, a member of our C team loved us so much that she broke ties with us first, in a most loving way, at great personal cost to herself. Taught us that it is ok to do the same. This break freed us, and I am so grateful.

The year leading up to the break — trying to keep all 40+ family members together and communicating the way we used to be — was horrible. Horrible. Lawyers and judges became involved. Hearts shattered. But since the break, we are lighter. We have so much more time. Our hearts are being healed by different people now. People who can listen to us without being hurt by us. And we find ourselves with the time again to be ourselves, finally, and to wish the same healing for the C team.

Nothing prepared us for this reality. We were lied to by a voice in our heads (our culture? our own fear?) that told us we _should_ be able to keep everyone together and that everyone _should_ care equally and _should_ contribute in similar ways or how we want them to contribute or in the exact same ways that they used to. That our wise, beloved father _should_ be strong enough not to allow his heartbreak and exhaustion and anger about slowly losing Mom to bleed into his relationships with others.

To that voice of fear in our heads, we now say "Bullshit." We have no time for Shoulds. I learned that it's perfectly ok, fabulous even, to let some people go for now. Some people offer us more by leaving, so we can focus where we need to. And we offer more to them by leaving, too.

Our small care partner team can be more flexible now. More free. We have to adapt to new realities daily now, sometimes hourly, sometimes by the minute. Much easier to do this as a lean, mean, care-partnering machine.

Sometimes the most loving choice you're left with is to let go of someone before anger hardens into contempt within you. If you are part of an Alzheimer's A team, or a lone care partner without your A team yet, you literally don't have time for contempt anymore. How cool is that? And in the moments you're really lucky, and you accept the break, you gain time to find new support.

It's possible to love people with your whole being and still say "Not my circus. Not my monkeys." Even to people who used to be your circus and your favorite monkeys. I love my C team members more now than ever and know that one day, likely after my parents pass, we will find and hug each other again. On the other hand, Mom and Dad have shut the door, likely for good, on the C team. It's all they can do. It is what it is. I've learned that I don't need to fix everything. Some broken things are just broken, and that's ok.

From my perspective, our A and C teams let go of each other over a year ago now. In hindsight, I wish we hadn't waited so long. I wish we hadn't hung on to old hopes and expectations as long as we did. We could have saved ourselves a year of inadvertently hurting each other. We could have opened this new time, this new rest, this new energy, for ourselves and our parents sooner. Found new companions and new help sooner. And began healing, sooner, too. After the break, life is still hard, but suddenly, life is sweet again.

Here at the center of the fire. Here where we live out our worst fears, year after year, and refuse to look away. Here within Team Jinda, life is beautiful.

Recognizing and Claiming Real Superpower #1: Finding Fun in All of the Above

Have you ever hit a point when you realized that a bunch of things you used to find enjoyable are just not that much fun for you anymore? What did you do about it?

In 2013, I hit that point again near the end of summer. The point of realizing that a large pile of things that used to be fun for me — things I gave a lot of time and love and energy to in the past — just weren't that much fun anymore. I felt it in my bones and it freaked me out. After all, if I gave up so many things that I used to do, what would be left of me? Who would I be now? Would I stop being me? Being fun? What would I do? How would I live now? And would any of my friends and family come with me?

Lori the Researcher showed up, as she tends to do when Go-With-the-Flow Lori's head starts to drown in overload. Lori the Researcher looked back into my own blog and compared all the posts from the summer of 2012 with those from the summer of 2013.

She confirmed that yes, in fact, what I found fun had shifted considerably. Researcher and Organizer People, please see the two remarkably concise, for me, tables at the end of this essay. Everybody else, feel free to roll your eyes at those tables and move on.

But I found something else too: something completely unexpected.

I found a person who had evolved beyond the fun and not fun polarities. I found a person who can, and often does, choose "Both" and "All of the above." Someone who can reimagine almost anything into fun. Holy shit! (I believe is the precise research term.)

I can now find the fun within the not fun. Most days.

I can find fun within almost anything that comes my way. Eventually, if not immediately. I'm still working on immediately.

Have you ever imagined with kids, friends or family about which superpowers you'd most like to have? Flying, x-ray vision, invisibility, that sort of thing?

For me, finding the fun in almost anything, most days, is the superpower I would choose. And, according to the data, says Lori The Researcher, I now have it.

This is big.

This means that I can stop worrying about letting go of my "no longer fun for me" things. I can stop worrying about most things, actually, when I remember that this real superpower is within me now.

I can let go of what no longer serves us. I can try the new. I can fail. Flail even. And so can the people I'm with.

Because even if we flail with no grace whatsoever, we can still laugh our asses off about it eventually, which is no small thing (the laughing, or our asses, your choice grammarians).

We will find the fun, even in the not fun.

I will find the fun as Go-With-The-Flow Lori, and as Researcher Lori, and as any other Loris that are needed and show up next.

Oh, these real superpowers are going to be so much fun!

Summer of 2012 Lori Experiences Documented in My Blog

This is fun!	This is not fun!
Writing	Worrying
Reflecting on giant questions asked by other people (for example, How do we trust each other without proof? How do we measure our freedom not using money? How do we create reflective communities where none seem to exist?)	Feeling off balance
Reflecting on our coworking space to answer giant questions	Oral surgery
Creating and defining new words	Not hearing from my mom after the release of our new book due to her Alzheimer's disease
Telling long-winded stories	Shootings/gun violence in our neighborhood
Welcoming newcomers into our space	Marketing
Documenting self-organizing groups in action	Talking about my own work (Always experienced as selling myself. Bleh.)
Improving and maintaining our home, yard, and garden	

Summer of 2013 Lori Experiences Documented in My Blog

Fun	Not fun	Both fun & not fun
Writing		
Spending unexpected time with family and finding new connection and community among my extended family	The death of a grandparent	X
Reflecting on my own questions (for example, How do I know I'm doing the right work? What is fun and not fun for me now?)	Work that stresses me out (involving over-busyness, deadlines, goals, and event planning) and work I feel I've just done to death (improving and maintaining our now too-large home, yard, and garden).	X
Talking about my own work	The word "marketing"	X
Asking for help	Asking for help	X
Following my own energy and stepping outside of my comfort zone	Stepping outside my own comfort zone, at first, as a result of following my own energy	X
Getting lost	Getting lost	X

Summer of 2013 Lori Experiences Documented in My Blog (continued)

Fun	Not fun	Both fun & not fun
Listening to and sharing the stories of people I love		
Noticing and mentioning the quiet, hidden courage in others		
Listening a lot and giving no more than 1 sentence of advice	Listening a lot and giving no more than 1 sentence of advice	X
Living as a writer	Living as a writer	X
Finding writer friends and colleagues	Finding writer friends and colleagues	X
Hanging out with friends, family, neighbors, and pets		
Self-publishing	Self-publishing	X

Even Neck Deep in Shit
I Am Glad for Your Company

A promise to my family...

****

Today, I will listen, not judge.

*Today, I will not trade in a deep ocean of love and respect
for the red-hot coal of contempt.*

*Today, I will forgive those who appear to judge me
and those who appear to choose narrow self-interest above love.*

*Today, when I mess this up again,
I will forgive myself
and start again.*

Because we are worth it.

****

I am making the choice today to love all beings
regardless of — and usually because of —
our faults and flaws.

We are not united in our perfection: we never were.

We are united in our imperfections.
Wise women say that the cracks are where the light can shine in:
and, boy, are we cracked.
They say that broken hearts are open hearts:
and, wow, are ours broken.

Yet, it was not before this, it is now — right now —
right in the middle of our own neck-deep-in-family-crap *now*
that we're becoming capable of infinite love.

I am capable of infinite love.

We can love beings

who are bickering,
being spiteful,
misremembering,
misrepresenting,
feeling contempt,
not seeing our perspective,
not wanting our help,
sticking their noses into places they don't belong,
lying or stealing,
and the worst, at least for me:
willfully rewriting a story of wholeness,
removing and forgetting the love,
the complexity of then, and the sheer simple beauty that is us,
even now.

We're all guilty of these things
at some point in our lives.
Forgiveness wouldn't work if we weren't all flawed.

****

Today, I will listen, not judge.

*Today, I will not trade in a deep ocean of love and respect
for the red-hot coal of contempt.*

*Today, I will forgive those who appear to judge me
and those who appear to choose narrow self-interest above love.*

*Today, when I mess this up again,
I will forgive myself
and start again.*

Because we are worth it.

****

Nasty actions are born from pain,
from fear, and sometimes
from exhaustion.

I believe
that scared beings, exhausted, in pain,
should be loved,
embraced,
forgiven.
I believe that being loved is
an inalienable right
of the living,
which even includes
the person I'd most like
to punch in the nose right now.

This is the way I was raised, family.
You raised me so well
that now my ears can hear
our long and winding story of wholeness
above this moment's name calling.
Now my eyes can see only
tired, sad, or scared humans when I am told
to fear the devil on the other side, by both sides.
Now my heart can only feel
an ocean of love and respect
for the people who brought me here. For you.
For all of you.

Your story is yours to tell. This one is mine.
In my story you are angels, capable of infinite love right now,
and you are also a giant pain in the ass,
capable of making me weep with frustration right now.
In my story, all of this is wanted and needed:
both angel wings and ass pain.
In my story, we are made more real to each other, and more whole,
in our brokenness together.
In my story, I would not trade a single one of you crazy people for
anyone or anything else on earth.

Even neck deep in shit, I am glad for your company.

If you look in my direction one day and the shit has covered my head entirely
know that unshakeable love for you is emanating outward
from somewhere inside that steaming pile.

I am in there remembering snow balls and swimming and fishing and sweet summer salads and songs around campfires.

I am in there recalling decades of your generosity, support, humor, and hugs — for both those who deserved it and those who didn't.

And I am 100 percent certain that when I reach out to find you again that your hand will find mine.

****

Today, I will listen, not judge.

Today, I will not trade in a deep ocean of love and respect for the red-hot coal of contempt.

Today, I will forgive those who appear to judge me and those who appear to choose narrow self-interest above love.

Today, when I mess this up again, I will forgive myself and start again.

Because we are worth it.

Almost Everything I Said in June Was Crap

This essay is a sister essay to No More To-Do Lists and Other Joys of Turning 45, found earlier in this book.

I wrote that essay in June 2015, just before my 45th birthday. It's October 2015, I'm now 45 ¼, and I'm so much wiser now. Really, it's scary how much wiser I am now. How full of crap June me seems now.

We're selling our Seattle home this month and — so we wouldn't completely lose our minds and tempers — last month we created a 65 line-item Google spreadsheet of all the things we have to do to prepare. We needed this to keep ourselves and friends on track and aware of what we and others were doing, and when. Without it, we'd have ended up yelling at each other for sure. If you thought that the No More To-Do Lists… essay meant I *never* make lists anymore, or if I did, we were both wrong.

We do make collective lists together now and then. We do so at the points life throws at us more than we can take and our heads begin swimming in details. We're not entirely magic non-busy beings yet. Maybe next year.

I noticed today, too, that my mantra is evolving. Apparently, the moment you become somewhat adept at regularly saying I Love You to most things each day and Fuck This to other things each day, and letting the rest go, and you start feeling pretty damn good about it, that's life's cue to start throwing bigger challenges your way.

For example, this month Daniel was laid off from his day job: the job that pays 98% of our bills and provides health "benefits" (good God my culture is stupid) making it possible for us to see our doctors, dentist, and eye doctor and to get medicine as needed. The same month my parents' new cottage on the island became suddenly available and we are flying to South Dakota and then driving their car across the country for them. The same month we're preparing our Seattle home and yard to sell. The same month this book is being edited, then published. The same month our cover illustrator had a major life event that meant she had to drop out for her own sake at the last minute when the covers were only 50% done. The same month my mom has been in the hospital multiple times again for stomach pain that the doctors are beginning to suspect may be Alzheimer's related: created and imagined by a failing brain.

What A Fucking Mess.

And yet, how lovely.

Daniel and I are planning a new life as artists and business partners together. Taking long morning walks together where deer and rabbits and sheep show up for us and we show up for them. Having staff meetings with the dog and cats on the sofa. We have even more time for people and work we love now.

And my parents will be living closer to us soon: I can't wait to have family close again!

And when the Seattle house sells, we won't have to be landlords anymore. Something we no longer want to be.

I love this fucking mess. My mess. My life.

I Love This Right-Now Too. I think I have a new mantra.

Epilogue: Gift #6: Becoming Respite

Early on, Mom's Alzheimer's disease was a fierce and terrible thing. A dragon come to burn our family to ash. Now and then, it can still feel that way. But the passing years broke us open too. And brought us power beyond our own imaginations.

I learned that we have it within us to break ourselves wide open and step out as someone new. Most days.

I learned that we have it within ourselves to shut ourselves off from the world, rest, and reassemble, other days.

I learned that we aren't just humans. We are dragons.

We aren't just burned. We are fire.

We aren't just victims. We are creators and story wranglers.

We aren't just wildly imperfect. We are perfectly, beautifully, human, too.

And I learned that we're not just stranded here, sinking with an incurable disease. We are groundless beings. We can everywhere.

Yes, that's a verb, friends. We can run, swim, fly, rest, hide, scream, recover, weep, change, laugh, imagine, and everywhere.

Thank you for everywhereing with me for a while...

Becoming Respite

I move in the world a changed being now

being now

today the yellow grass in the field up the hill is bowing to the rain
the sea and the land and the sky cede their colors into fog,
becoming one
passing waxwings eat red berries off the vine, laugh at the cat
gray waves crash into the shore, laughing too

then there's me
powerful and helpless beyond imagination
standing in the rain drenched
crying at the beauty of it all

respite is not a thing we are given
respite is who we are right now
bowing to the moment together

respite is who we're becoming
allowing our true selves to be

— Lori, October 9, 2015, Whidbey Island, WA

About the Author

Lori Kane is a writer, poet, Alzheimer's care partner, and coworking space creator. She's serious about home canning and collecting driftwood and stones on beach walks. Aspires to playfulness in all other things. Lori lives on Whidbey Island, Washington, USA with husband and creative partner-in-crime Daniel Gregory, Eva the dog, and Joe, Bella, and Batman the cats.

The essays and poetry in this book reflect her family's decade-long experience of living with Alzheimer's disease. To find her other books, visit her website at www.collectiveself.com, stop by for a chat on her Lori Kane, Author Facebook page, or follow her @CollectiveSelf on Twitter.

This photo was taken by Daniel. His work can be found at www.danieljgregory.com. He's awesome. Check it out.

Acknowledgements

Thank you Daniel for continuing to support me through all the ups and downs of being a care partner, an indie author, a creator, a dragon, and a human.

Thank you Mary "The Canning Monster" for being a great neighbor, friend, and editor.

Thank you mom Linda, dad Jim, sister Jen, brother-in-law Cam, and all the rest of my family and friends for allowing me write what I need to write, when I need to write it, with the awareness that I'll be supported, loved, and forgiven regularly, or at least eventually, as needed.

Thank you poet Jericho Brown for writing a poem that inspired me to be far more trusting and vulnerable in writing than I'd ever been before. And the women of Hedgebrook for introducing me to his work.

Thank you Knox for going through dementia hell and dementia heaven in a parallel universe to my own and continuing to demonstrate how to survive, and be funny doing so, the whole way down and up and down and up and down and up again.

Thank you Isaac for stepping in and creating book covers at a moment's notice. Isaac is awesome. See more of his work here: http://isaacnovak.com.

Thank you Marigrace, and the whole UW Medicine Memory & Brain Wellness Center, for inviting me into your world and allowing me to see that people outside my own circles might be interested in a book like this.

Thank you Robyn, and the whole staff, at The Regency on Whidbey for helping make my parent's new home feel like home.

Thank you other care partners who magically create time for writing. Karen and Kim, care partners and In Care of Dad bloggers. Other Karen, care partner and Missing Jim blogger. Holly Hughes, care partner and editor of the book *Beyond Forgetting, Poetry and Prose* about Alzheimer's Disease. And so many, many others. You somehow make time for yourselves, your families, your writing, and your world: making you pure gold and pure magic to me. Thank you for your work and for living so openly.

You are all gifts beyond measure.

Other Books by Lori Kane

Reimagination Station:
Creating a Game-Changing In-Home Coworking Space

The book, which was created flash-style in four weeks, is an invaluable tool for home coworking hosts. It's also a rich resource for anyone who wants to grow the connectedness of neighborhoods, create something beautiful and valuable that isn't driven by profit, and extend themselves further into their community.

Cat Johnson, Sharable Magazine

Year 1 Poet

Thank you for such wonderful words to remember. My gratitude is endless today because of you.

Sue Reed, a Reader

Different Office: Stories from Self-Created, Soul-Satisfying Work Space

All in all, Different Office, for all its gently humorous and deeply personal explorations of alternative workplaces, is a seminal book. It documents actual, viable alternatives. It takes the idea of work one step further towards fun.

Bernie DeKoven, Game Designer, Author, Lecturer and Fun Theorist

A Travel Guide for Transitions: Because Freaking Out About This by Myself Totally Sucks

This book has given me the inspiration and ideas on how to be ok with me, the weirdness, the sucky days, and come out ok. I love it – a great read for anyone who feels lost in life or just wants to read about how others are overcoming "normal life" and finding something fantastic by following what they love. The book is packed with whimsical illustrations that really add to the stories and make for a fun easy read.

Tabitha Borchardt, Artist and Avid Reader

Different Work: Moving from I Should to I Love My Work

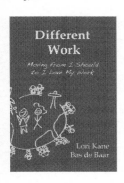

I so related to the Three Amigos story. Their story gave me lots of hope and encouragement to continue the journey.

You are an inspiration for folks who are doing the work they love and for those who would like to do the work they love.

Dr. Cathy Fromme, TrustWorks